Routledge Revivals

Age of Fear

First published in 2004 in the immediate wake of the September 11 terrorist attacks, this is an accessible commentary intended to provoke thought and debate on the topic of terrorism. In a collection of challenging essays, questions consider the causes of terrorism and why post-modern terrorism is different. The essays are divided into three key sections, first investigating the civilizational roots and dimensions of contemporary terrorism, next examining the Bush administration's approach, and finally, considering the complex and changing relationship between fear and freedom. Written by a leading scholar in Middle East and Asian Studies, this comprehensive reissue will be of particular value to students of international relations and terrorism studies, as well as the more general reader with an interest in the global issues faced in the age of contemporary terrorism.

Age of Fear

Power versus Principle in the War on Terror

Amitav Acharya

First published in 2004
by Marshall Cavendish Academic

This edition first published in 2014 by Routledge
2 Park Square, Milton Park, Abingdon, Oxon, OX14 4RN

Simultaneously published in the USA and Canada
by Routledge
711 Third Avenue, New York, NY 10017

Routledge is an imprint of the Taylor & Francis Group, an informa business

Publisher's Note
The publisher has gone to great lengths to ensure the quality of this reprint but points out that some imperfections in the original copies may be apparent.

Disclaimer
The publisher has made every effort to trace copyright holders and welcomes correspondence from those they have been unable to contact.

A Library of Congress record exists under LOC control number: 2005345614

ISBN 13: 978-0-415-73289-5 (hbk)
ISBN 13: 978-1-315-84881-5 (ebk)
ISBN 13: 978-0-415-73291-8 (pbk)

AMITAV ACHARYA

AGE OF FEAR

POWER VERSUS PRINCIPLE IN THE WAR ON TERROR

Published 2004 by Marshall Cavendish Academic
An imprint of Marshall Cavendish International (Singapore) Private Limited
A member of Times Publishing Limited

Times Centre, 1 New Industrial Road,
Singapore 536196
Tel:(65) 6213 9288
Fax: (65) 6284 9772
E-mail: mca@sg.marshallcavendish.com
Website:
http://www.marshallcavendish.com/academic

ISBN: 981-210-340-6

A CIP catalogue record for this book is available from the National Library Board (Singapore).

Printed by Times Graphics Pte Ltd, Singapore
on non-acidic paper

London • New York • Beijing • Shanghai • Bangkok • Kuala Lumpur • Singapore

Contents

Preface: Like All Ordinary Mortals

On September 11, 2001, a group of terrorists from the Middle East attacked the World Trade Center and the Pentagon. Using a novel tactic, they hijacked civilian airliners to use as missiles to crash into the huge edifices that served as the most powerful icons of American economic and military power. Two planes were used to destroy the Twin Towers of the World Trade Center, another to inflict massive damage to an entire section of the Pentagon. A fourth plane, on its way to either the US Congress or the White House, crashed in Pennsylvania when its passengers found out what was going on and struggled with the hijackers in the cockpit. Over 4,000 people—mainly Americans—died in the attacks, especially at the World Trade Center.

This catastrophic event marked the end of the "post-Cold War era" in international relations. It has brought about a profound change in America's foreign policy and its relations with the outside world. It has led the Bush administration to launch a global war on terror centred on the Middle East and Asia, as well as on its own home front. America has embarked on a new course of foreign interventionism and global policing which the Bush administration had forsworn when it was elected into office. The administration, already no believer in multilateralism, has retreated from it even further since the September 11 attacks. Moreover, the attacks have produced the most sweeping changes in American domestic security in recent history, which other countries are emulating.

This book is my attempt to make sense of these changes.

Like all ordinary people, I am in mortal fear of terrorists, especially since September 11, 2001. Every time I board a plane, or step into a pub in Holland Village in Singapore, Bangsar in Kuala Lumpur, or Sukhumvit in Bangkok, or walk the wonderfully chaotic streets of Bangkok, Jakarta and Delhi, I wonder whether I could be a victim of the next terrorist attack. I was saddened, frightened and angered by the September 11 attacks on the United States. I strongly supported the US led war to oust the Taliban regime in Afghanistan and felt compelled to write an op-ed (published in the *International Herald Tribune* and included in this volume) to dismiss the view that this war (not Iraq) would spark a clash of civilizations against America. I have zero sympathy for terrorists, no matter where they come from, how valid their cause, and how righteous their anger. I make absolutely no apologies for any group—Hindus, Muslims, Christians, Palestinians, Tamils, Afghans, and Irish—that kills innocent citizens, under whatever pretext. I expect and hope that governments, in cooperation with their own citizens and the international community, will do their best to eradicate the menace of international terrorism. In this endeavour, they deserve the support of all peace-loving and justice-seeking people.

But every concerned person has a right to know a few basic truths about the "war on terror" and ask whether the way the war is being conducted by the United States and its allies is necessarily the best and the only way to defeat the threat.

Terrorism, especially the possibility of terrorists using weapons of mass destruction is a grave danger. But is terrorism the most serious threat to humankind in "our time" as some Bush administration officials put it? Millions of people fall victim every day to other sources of insecurity, including hunger, disease and repression, and not just in the so-called Third World. I find it hard to accept the claim that poverty, humiliation and lack of democracy have less to do with terrorism, compared to, say, Islamic ideology or Al-Qaeda.

Having followed closely the way the Bush administration justified and conducted the war against Iraq, and the subsequent failure of coalition forces to uncover any weapons of mass destruction in Iraq, one would have less faith in a government's ability to tell the truth about the need for military action in the name of fighting terror. One is not sure if the Bush administration, or some of its allies, are really above using the war on terror for political advantage. I believe a different Republican president, or a Democrat, might have handled the threat posed by terrorism with more nuance and in a manner less damaging to international order. I fear that even after the Iraqi intelligence fiasco, governments will still be tempted to manipulate intelligence information and exploit the public's concern with terrorism to push for political goals that have little to do with terrorism. The Saddam regime was heinous and deserving of being overthrown through foreign military intervention. But any such intervention should and could have been undertaken collectively after the UN inspectors had a further chance to conduct their investigations. Does the timing of the war and the manner of its organization, whatever the aggravation, justify the serious long-term damage to international order that resulted from it?

The essays in the book are divided into three main sections. **Culture, Fear and the Roots of Terror** investigates the alleged civilizational roots and dimensions of contemporary terrorism. This section examines how the "clash of civilizations" thesis has fared in the light of September 11. Is civilization a more useful category than state or society in understanding the sources of terror and explaining responses to it? Is religion the real impulse behind contemporary terrorism, more so than politics or the Palestinian injustice? Is terrorism more localized than what a civilization framework would connote? Would it better to view militant Islam as a clash within a civilization? Can we blame all and any forms of terrorism on Muslim extremism or view them as aftershocks of September 11? While Southeast Asia shows that the roots of terror are as much local as they are linked to a global network, Southeast Asia also shows that the link between terrorism and other forms of internal conflict predates September 11 and cannot be blamed entirely on Muslim radicalism or religious teaching.

America's Fears and the Fear of America examines the Bush administration's approach to terrorism. I make a firm distinction between "America" and the Bush administration. I do not believe that the Bush Doctrine, its underlying neo-con ideology, and the conduct of the Iraq War are quintessentially "American". They may be more than a passing moment in history, but it will be a mistake to take the unilateralist impulse, the pre-emptive strategy and the politics of mass deception that produced the war against Iraq as a permanent transformation in the American psyche. America remains and, I argue, will remain a spring board for alternative pathways once the current paranoia subsides.

Politics and Principles in the Age of Fear deals with the complex and changing relationship between fear and freedom. This section examines how the "freedom for fear" campaign as defined by the Bush administration translates into a fear of the freedoms that had hitherto defined America's identity and foreign policy approach. It looks at the impact of terrorism and counter-terrorism on prospects for democracy at home and abroad. Also examined is the question of how the war on terror has affected some of the basic principles of international order espoused by key states in the West and Asia, for example Australia, in relation to multilateralism and India in relation to non-alignment. How has the war on terror affected Asian security strategies and order?

This is not an academic book on terrorism. To be sure, many of the essays deal with such questions as: Who is a terrorist? How is post-modern (as defined below in the first essay) terrorism different? Who are the victims? Most important, what causes terrorism? But while most terrorism experts are concerned with finding answers to these questions, my aim is to problematize them. The answers to all these questions are, and ought to be, contested. And this contested understanding of just who you should be protected from is an integral aspect of the Age of Fear.

Given the importance of the topic, it is not surprising that scholarship of terrorism has become as opportunistic as many members of America's "coalition of the willing". In the Age of Fear, the gap between analysis and action has become increasingly blurred. I have often marvelled at the rapidity with which "experts" on terrorism have appeared on the scene after the September 11 attacks, sometimes by simply relabelling their previous work on war and violence. But then, we live in an Age of Fear and fear legitimizes scholarship that would be untenable in happier times.

Without pretending to be a terrorism scholar or analyst, I wrote these essays as a student of international relations with a special interest in Asia and the Middle East. They are about how September 11 has altered the world in which we live. What the reader will find in this book is not a comprehensive and in-depth analysis of the causes and consequences of terrorism or technical discussion of counter-terrorism strategies adopted by governments. Rather they will find here personal reflections on how September 11, 2001 has changed our world. The fears described here are real; they are shared worldwide. The principles at stake are universal ones. If these essays can raise awareness of the importance of defending the principles being undermined by the Age of Fear, I would consider this to be a worthy contribution.

The presentation of the essays in the volume does not follow a chronological sequence. Rather, the chapters are thematically organized into the "three fears" that the book talks about. I have also made no attempt to update the original articles and papers. This is meant to give the reader a sense of my perspective at the time of the various unfolding events. The book covers the events of roughly a two-year period, from September 11, 2001 to the end of 2003, perhaps the most critical years in our descent into the Age of Fear.

Acknowledgements

The author gratefully acknowledges Deborah Lee, Kamal Siddhu, Karyn Wang and Amle Gouri Gopal for research assistance and Arabinda Acharya for help with South Asian terrorist organizations and Indo-US security relations.

Fear: A painful emotion or passion excited by the expectation of evil, or the apprehension of impending danger; apprehension; anxiety; solicitude; alarm; dread.
http://www.selfknowledge.com/35217.htm

"We fear flying, we fear travelling, we fear certain countries, we fear certain religions, we fear certain people, we fear the shoes they wear, we fear cargo ships, imported goods, letters and parcels—in fact we fear everything around us…we are going to feel this fear and the consequences for a very long time."
Mahathir Mohamad, speaking at the 11th Annual Meeting of the Asia Pacific Parliamentary Forum.

1

Age of Fear

The new "post-September 11 era" is an Age of Fear. International relations is now not just about power politics but also about fear politics. We live in a world where power is no longer an adequate guarantee against fear. In fact, power begets fear. The more powerful a nation is, the more fearful it becomes.

The US is the most powerful nation on earth. But September 11 has also made it the most fearful nation. This apparently contradictory combination, awesome power and unprecedented fear, is profoundly reshaping the international security order. Above all, it has ushered in a conflict between American power politics and some of the core principles of international order including principles of just war, respect for the rule of law and collective security.

Power and Fear Politics

	Power politics	Fear politics
Main enemy	State/s	Transnational terror networks
Nature of threat	Aggression (mainly military)	Intimidation (mainly psychological)
Security concept	National security	Homeland security
International security cooperation	Multilateral	Ad hoc, "Coalition of the Willing"

The post-September 11 era is defined by three principal kinds of fear.

The first kind of fear is the most obvious one. Terrorism of course has a long history, but its nature, sources, and implications are changing. One of the more succinct descriptions of the new and "post-modern" terrorism came from Singapore Minister for Trade and Industry, George Yeo:

> The new terrorism is of a different genre. Like in a civil war, the threat is harder to pinpoint because it is within. Families may be split with the 'good' and the 'bad' mixed together. It is globalized by the same technologies which created the global economy. It does not consist of guerillas sheltering in the countryside making occasional incursions into the cities, but operates and draws strengths in multi-ethnic and multireligious urban environments. It makes use of air travel and the Internet. It uses similar encryption algorithms to hide its internal communications. Worst of all, its members are prepared to die for their cause.

Every time a new terrorist act takes place, our conception of what terrorism is and how it threatens us changes. September 11 was a turning point in the sense that planes were used as missiles in suicide missions. The targets were the very symbols of American military and economic supremacy. The Bali bombings of October 12, 2002 turned our attention to "soft" targets: the Western tourists and the entertainment spots they patronise. Terrorism targets the hegemon and its allies. It also targets states who are not allies of the hegemon but are destinations for its citizens as tourists. Terrorists have at once become more varied and more specific in choosing their targets.

After New York and Bali, came Mombasa. This was a failed attempt in which terrorists—suspected to be from either Osama bin Laden's Al-Qaeda or one of the components of his International Islamic Front (IIF)—tried to shoot down an Israeli chartered plane carrying Israeli tourists with the help of two missiles fired from the ground, as it was taking off from the Mombasa airport in Kenya. The plane and its passengers escaped, but the incident underscored another terrorist tactics, which have been evolving at least since the 1980s.

The anti-Soviet war in Afghanistan in the 1980s saw the use of the US-supplied Stinger missiles against Soviet aircraft and gunship helicopters. Amongst terrorist organizations, the Chechens, and the Liberation Tigers of Tamil Eelam (LTTE) of Sri Lanka have this capability. The intelligence and security agencies of many countries, including India, have been very concerned about such threats. While in the past such capabilities have been used mainly against military aircraft, the Mombasa episode took terrorism to new heights.

Both Bali and Mombasa were seen by terrorism exports as inspired by bin Laden's threat in his message that was broadcast through Al Jazeera on November 12, 2002, to damage the Western economy. Such strikes were directed against the global economy, not just that of Indonesia or Kenya. The strikes were meant to create a fear of travel. Terrorists are targeting the travel industry and its means of transport. The bombing of the Mariott Hotel in Jakarta increased such fears. Terrorist strikes in other places: Istanbul, Madrid, and Riyadh, have contributed to the perception of terrorism further spreading its tentacles and acquirine new targets and adopting new strategies.

Adding considerably to the fear of post-modern terror is the fear of weapons of mass destruction, as articulated in Bush's axis of evil formulation. The terrorist can kill not in hundreds, but in thousands and millions. Many analysts today believe that it's only a matter of time before a chemical or biological attack is carried out against the US, possibly within the US, or even that a crude nuclear device will be used for this purpose. This kind of fear was underscored in Bush's opening salvo in the 2004 presidential campaign.

A scared America has turned scary.

The second trend of fear we live in today is the fear of the hegemon. American power—including its unrivalled hard power and the Bush administration's exercise of it, the doctrine of pre-emption, the neo-con ideology and its disregard for multilateralism—define the second kind of fear that marks our age. The first of these elements was brought home by the swift and decisive nature of the US military victory over the Taliban. It took the US barely a month to decimate its much-vaunted adversary. Many experts had thought that the US counter-strike in Afghanistan would be a prolonged, difficult and ultimately unwinnable campaign. How could the US win a war in which the target was so elusive and unidentifiable? Didn't Afghanistan have a history of humiliating foreign invaders? Afghanistan offered a resounding demonstration of the "new American way of war". This is warfare centred upon weapons with capabilities to achieve extremely

Significant Terrorist Attacks Since September 11th
(From September 2001 to June 2004)

	Date	Location	Description
1	13.12.2001	New Delhi, India	Suicide terrorist attack on the Indian parliament in New Delhi. 12 persons including 5 terrorists were killed and 22 injured.
2	11.4.2002	Djerba, Tunisia	Explosion at ancient synagogue in Tunisia leaves 17 dead, including 11 German tourists.
3	8.5.2002	Karachi, Pakistan	Car explodes outside hotel in Karachi, Pakistan, killing 14, including 11 French citizens.
4	14.6.2002	Karachi, Pakistan	Bomb explodes outside American Consulate in Karachi, Pakistan, killing 12.
5	6.10.2002	Yemen	A small boat loaded with explosives hit the Linburg tanker, causing an oil spill and fires.
6	12.10.2002	Bali, Indonesia	Explosions destroyed two popular nightclubs in Bali. The death toll was set at 202, including citizens from 21 countries.
7	22.10.2002	Moscow, Russian Federation	Chechen terrorists took 800 people hostage in the Moscow theatre hostage crisis. 129 died in the rescue effort.
8	28.11.2002	Mombasa, Kenya	Two handheld missiles were fired at an Israeli Arkia airliner passenger plane. Meanwhile, terrorists crash an explosives-filled vehicle into a hotel in Mombasa, killing themselves and 16 others and injuring 80.

Significant Terrorist Attacks Since September 11th
(From September 2001 to June 2004) (cont'd)

9	27.12.2002	Chechnya Government, Grozny	Vehicles with explosives smashed through security barriers of the government building, killing 72 and injuring 210.
10	12.5.2003	Riyadh, Kindgom of Saudi Arabia	Four explosions rocked housing compounds for Westerners in Riyadh, Saudi Arabia. Suicide bombers killed 34, and injured 194.
11	16.5.2003	Casablanca, Morocco	Four car bombs targeting Jewish, Spanish and Belgian sites killed 24 people, in Morocco's commercial capital Casablanca.
12	4.7.2003	Quetta, Pakistan	Suicide bombers carried out an attack on a Muslim Shiite mosque in south-western Quetta, and caused 52 deaths.
13	1.8.2003	Mozdok, Russian Federation	Fifty people were killed and around 72 were injured when a suspected separatist Chechen rebel drove his truck loaded with explosives into a military hospital.
14	5.8.2003	Jakarta, Indonesia	13 people died and 149 were injured in a blast at the Marriott Hotel in Jakarta, allegedly carried out by Jemaah Islamiyah.
15	19.8.2003	Baghdad, Iraq	A bomb-laden truck exploded at the UN representative's office, killing Sergio Vieira de Mello and 16 others, and injuring 40.

Significant Terrorist Attacks Since September 11th
(From September 2001 to June 2004) (cont'd)

16	8.11.2003	Riyadh, Saudi Arabia	Al-Qaeda suicide bombers attacked a Riyadh residential compound of foreigners, leaving 30 dead.
17	15.11.2003	Istanbul, Turkey	Car bombs exploded outside two Istanbul synagogues, killing 20 and injuring 257.
18	20.11.2003	Istanbul, Turkey	Two suicide truck bombings targeted at the London-based HSBC building and the British embassy saw at least 27 killed including the British Consul General and wounded 450.
19	11.3.2004	Madrid, Spain	The Madrid attacks kill 40 when three trains were hit by near-simultaneous explosions.
20	29.5.2004	Saudi Arabia	In a series of attacks, terrorists targeted petroleum offices, a public bus, and an expatriate housing compound over two days, and killed 18 people including 7 foreigners.

long ranges, to reach targets with unparalleled precision, and to capitalize on gigabytes of positioning information gathered on the ground, in the air and from space. In this war, airpower, backed by target-spotting special forces, surveillance aircraft and imaging satellites with electronic systems and sensors able to peer through darkness and clouds, play a decisive role.

This new American Way of War is also thoroughly "smart". In the 1991 Gulf War only 10 per cent of the bombs were precision-guided, meaning they could sense and hit targets from a laser beam or pick up signals from a Global Positioning System (GPS) satellite. In the Afghan War, 90 per cent of the bombs were thus capable. The main precision-guided weapon in the Gulf War was a cruise missile costing US$1 million apiece. In Afghanistan, the main weapon of the air war was a kit, called the Joint Direct Attack Munition (JDAM), which could make dumb bombs smart by attaching a GPS and tail fins to guide a bomb 16 kilometres from the aircraft to the target. It came at a cost of US$18,000 each.

The war in Iraq was even more technologically impressive. This was the war in which the so-called information warfare came of age. The heroes of this war were Command, Control, Communications, Computing, Intelligence, Surveillance, and Reconnaissance (C4ISR) technology, space surveillance satellites, airborne Joint Surveillance and Target Attack Radar Systems (JSTARS) and unmanned aerial vehicles (UAVs). The technology allowed coalition forces to deliver an integrated, real-time, optical, infra-red, and radar picture on static ground objects and enemy vehicular and troop movement. It magnified the lethality of precision attack systems such as cruise missiles, Army Tactical Missile Systems (ATACMs), JDAMs, and High Speed Anti-Radiation Missiles (HARMs). The shock and awe campaign enabled the America-led coalition-achieved victory at a cost of just over 100 casualties, half the time of the first Gulf War, and with a third of the troops.

Aside from its military might, the fear of America owes to its diplomatic tack. Now that the unipolar "moment" has turned out to be a full-blown unipolar "era", the issue of peace and freedom is now closely bound up with that of US strategic primacy. And the American way of managing international order under the Bush administration has helped to ushar the new global fear politics.

Dashing initial hopes and calls for a renewed commitment to multilateralism, George W. Bush did not replicate the "New World Order" approach that his father had employed against Saddam Hussein in 1990. Instead of collective security, he invoked the right of national self-defence under the UN charter to bypass direct Security Council authorization for the conduct of the military campaign. Learning from Kosovo where alliance warfare had proven cumbersome, the US also shunned NATO's direct involvement, although the alliance had invoked its collective defence provision for the first time in history in the aftermath of the September 11 attacks.. While the international community was generally supportive of the US position, each of America's key regional allies demanded and secured something in return for their backing for the US. China and Russia were quick to press for an American understanding that domestic insurgencies should be viewed as a terrorist, rather than as a human rights issue. India secured American backing for its own war against terrorism involving Pakistani-supported Kashmir militants.

Multilateralism was pushed further into retreat by the neo-imperial ideology of the Bush administration. This ideology was aptly summed up by William Kristol, editor of the Washington, DC-based political magazine, the *Weekly Standard*: "We're going to get criticized for being an imperial power anyway, so you might as well make sure that the good guys win". Originally socialists or liberals who opposed the Vietnam War, the neo-cons are a bunch of disillusioned patriots who parted company with the traditional conservatives who argue for an isolationist posture for America. The neo-cons advocate a more activist and interventionist foreign policy. Aside from Kristol, this group includes key administration officials such as Deputy Secretary of Defense Paul Wolfowitz and Lewis Libby, National Security Adviser to Vice President Dick Cheney. Aided by flagship publications such as the *Weekly Standard* and *Commentary*, and backed by the *Wall Street Journal*, *National Review* and others, the neo-cons are defined by several core attributes. Briefly put, they want empire, dismiss international law and institutions ("America is so strong, it can safely ignore other nations"), show little regard for constitutional freedoms, endorse more Israeli settlements on the West Bank, and favour containment of China.

In sum, the fear of America is not a fear of American going around attacking all and sundry nations. Rather this is a fear of irresponsible and self-serving American foreign and security policy aggravating the very threats and challenges it promises to protect us from. If military powers and ideology creates the second kind of fear, a third type of fear unleashed by September 11 stems from the doctrine of homeland security. What George Bush describes as a battle between fear and freedom can be seen in the perverse context of fearful democracies retreating from the very freedoms they seek to defend against the terrorists. In America as elsewhere, freedom from fear reinforces the fear of freedoms.

After September 11, fewer people talk about the "end of the nation state". Instead, we hear a lot more about control over borders, control of financial flows, fingerprinting at airport immigration. We hear and talk about security doctrines that promise all-encompassing surveillance of all aspects of our lives. Responses to September 11 have led to the retreat of democracy and human rights both in the East and the West.

Poor Francis Fukuyama. His "end of history" thesis argued that the end of the Cold War had resulted in the "final" victory for liberal democracy and free markets, with no further contestations over ideas about, and approaches to, world order. The Fukuyama thesis strengthened the proponents of the Kantian "democratic peace" asserting that a world of liberal democracies would enjoy greater peace and pre-empt any clash of civilizations. This debate has been overtaken by September 11. Fukuyama has been challenged by the emergence of a new paradigm of global fear politics in which states are reasserting themselves over societal forces and liberal democracy is in some retreat. The new fear of terrorism goes hand in hand with a renewed fear of the state.

The post-September 11 fear was brought to the surface by a report of the US Justice Department's inspector general, who serves as an internal watchdog. The report reviews the handling of 762 illegal immigrants who were jailed in the immediate aftermath of September 11 attacks on the World Trade Center and the Pentagon, as part of a general sweep of potential suspects who might carry out another attack. (None were charged as terrorists and most have been deported). The report found that many people had no connection to terrorism. They were held for long periods without being told of the charges against them and were subjected to "unduly harsh" conditions of confinement. The report found "significant problems" in their treatment, including continuous lock-up, being moved around in handcuffs and leg irons, and having their cell lights kept on day and night. "While our review recognized the enormous challenges and difficult circumstances confronting the department in responding to the terrorist attacks, we found significant problems in the way the detainees were handled". Commenting on the report, ACLU Executive Director Anthony Romero said: "This Justice Department report will corroborate much of what we've been saying for 18 months ... The war on terrorism quickly turned into a war on immigrants".

Writing in *The Economist* magazine, Harold Hungjo Koh, Clinton's Assistant Secretary of State for Human Rights, argues: "Around the globe, America's human rights policy has visibly softened, subsumed under the all-encompassing banner of the 'war against terrorism'. And at home, the Patriot Act, military commissions, Guantanamo and the indefinite detention of American citizens have placed America in the odd position of condoning deep intrusions by law, even while creating zones and persons outside the law". He cites a number of actions such as the creation of a "total information awareness" programme under which the government may gather information about citizens and access records—telephone, financial, educational, medical—without showing evidence of involvement in terrorism. Koh believes that these setbacks are temporary, but one cannot be so sure. The fact is that measures undertaken by governments to strengthen security against terrorism can end up making states and their peoples even more insecure, whether deliberately or not.

The Age of Fear presents all of us with unpleasant choices. Addressing one type of fear solely on its own terms can aggravate the other types. For example, American leadership is needed in combating the fear of the terrorist, but the price may be an increased fear of the hegemon. To overcome the fear of the terrorist, you need homeland security, but it creates another kind of fear, fear of the surveillance state.

Total Fear

Terrorism, a senior Pentagon official recently asserted in Singapore, is "the greatest threat to peace in our time".

Really? To those who are old enough, or not-so-old enough, to remember President Ronald Reagan, wasn't communism, represented by the then "evil empire" of the Soviet Union, supposed to be the greatest threat to peace in the world?

Never mind. The discourse on terrorism and its sources has become increasingly homogenizing and totalizing. This totalizing representation holds Islamic radicalism as the main cause of global terror and Al-Qaeda, a global shadowy network, as its main agent. This view dismisses, or even mocks, poverty and the Palestinian issue as causes of terror. It seldom acknowledges local roots and agents of terror, or the link between local grievances and the upsurge of terrorism. Instead, it puts network and transnational reach at the centre of the threat.

The totalizing discourse on terror also blurs the distinction between terrorism drawing upon religious fundamentalism and other forms of political violence, such as those linked to ethnic rivalry, and demands for self-determination. Even in terrorist acts that are based on religious ideology, it fails to distinguish acts of revenge brought about by humiliation and alienation (as in the case of the Palestinian suicide bombers in Gaza), from terrorist acts fuelled by ideological aspirations for an Islamic superstate (as espoused by the Jemaah Islamiah, or JI, network).

The totalizing discourse on terror has its basis in the forces of globalization at work. Terrorist groups may have local roots, but their effectiveness is largely due to their opportunity to network and draw support from counterparts in other parts of the world.

Consider the Aum Shinrikyo group in Japan, whose leader, Shoko Asahara, was given the death sentence in late February 2004 for the group's role in the Tokyo subway gas attacks in the 1990s. Although its target was the Tokyo subway, it is hardly a "Japanese" group. Its members included many Russians. It tested its weapons on a farm in Western Australia. It maintained contacts with groups in the US to learn about making chemical weapons. It had an office in the US. The Maoists in Nepal have similar offices in US and Europe.

But the totalizing discourse of terrorism is driven more by the politics of representation than of reality. It's a way for states and intellectual elites to collectively frame and securitize widely disparate causes into a single policy project, which makes it easier to legitimize.

Yet, the price for this is a distortion of our understanding about what causes terrorism and blinds us to the responses needed. Consider the search for terror's "root causes", a term that has become one of the most meaningless clichés in contemporary international relations. This is part of the totalizing discourse. Different leaders and experts debate whether poverty, the Palestinian issue, alienation, or lack of political space is the root cause of radical Islamic ideology. This is cast in either-or terms.

The JI members held in detention in Singapore since December 2001 are neither poor nor illiterate. The Aum Shinrikyo members in Japan were like "ordinary Japanese", well-educated men from a middle-class background. Does it therefore mean that poverty is not a root cause of terrorism, as some assert? Yet, the Naxalite terrorism in India feeds from poverty; one of their areas of operation is Orissa, India's poorest state.

Lack of political space may not be a root cause of terrorism in Japan, but it is certainly so in Egypt and much of the Middle East. It is also a root cause of Maoist terror in Nepal and in Burma.

Radical Islamic ideology, disseminating partly from Saudi-funded religious and educational institutions, may be a root cause of terror in Southeast Asia but it certainly is not in Sri Lanka and Nepal. The Maoists in Nepal are mostly non-Hindu (they are backed by tribal groups which are Buddhists).

The most severe forms of terrorism, such as suicide terrorism, were developed not by Islamic groups, but by the Hindu LTTE.

The personal messianic charisma of the leader is a key factor behind terrorism sponsored by the LTTE, Aum and Al-Qaeda. But more mundane leaders who exploit the material grievances of their communities have led many other terrorist campaigns, such as that in Nepal and India. The search for root causes will not lead to meaningful conclusions without acknowledging these variations. The totalizing discourse on terrorism not only distorts our understanding of the causes of terror, but also responses to it. It leads to a single strategic approach, focusing on intelligence-sharing, training, etc.

Globalization and communications advances give terrorist groups an opportunity to network with other groups and draw sustenance and support. But to acknowledge this is not to hype terrorism as the single most important threat affecting us worldwide. This would mean neglecting other challenges, and security concerns, both global and local, which threaten us more seriously.

The totalizing tendency is not just evident in the Bush administration's view of the scale (as a global threat) and intensity (as the most serious threat) of the terrorist threat, but also in the kind of responses needed to combat this menace. It harks back to the Cold War, when the US tended to view all regional security problems from the single prism of superpower rivalry and the evil empire of the Soviet Union. One consequence, as we well know now, was the Taliban.

Just as terrorism is presented as a single overarching global threat, the war on terror is conceptualized and waged as a single worldwide campaign. Yet, some elements of what is presented as the war on terror are genuine, while others are phony. Many people, this author included (as the essay: "Why this was not a clash of civilizations", indicates) supported the war against the Taliban. But many of the same people, again including this author, refused to support the US attack on Iraq because they found its justification phony, even though the Bush administration presented both these actions as being part of the war on terror. What seemed genuine and urgent in the case of Taliban seemed self-serving and arrogant in the case of Iraq.

Representing dissenting news on the "war on terror" is not to dismiss terrorism as a highly dangerous threat to our security and well-being. It certainly is. But the purpose of dissent is to reject the tendency to conflate all sorts of challenges under a single overarching framework and to encourage a search for alternative understandings of terrorism and responses to it.

Overcoming Fear

Can the international community work together to combat terrorism and end the Age of Fear? In seeking answers to this question, we need to bear in mind the various forces at work in shaping the war on terror: culture, power, freedom, and international principles (norms). Culture matters in determining whether September 11 would develop into a clash of civilizations as predicted by Samuel Huntington. The question of power relates to the power of the US as it conducts the war on terrorism, re-engineers its alliances and relates to the rest of the world in developing an anti-terror coalition. The question of freedom is important given the way in which responses to September 11 have led to the retreat of democracy and human rights both in the East and the West. Finally, international norms will affect what sort of cooperation against terrorism will develop and how legitimate such cooperation will be.

September 11 underscored and accentuated the diversity of views not only with regard to the nature, sources and dimensions of terrorism, but also responses to it. This diversity, reflecting both domestic and external security concerns of states, has shaped their choice between principle and opportunism, and between national interest and common interest. It has also shaped their relations with the US, which, in turn, affects the prospect for international cooperation again fear.

Governments throughout the world have not shied away from exploiting the September 11 for political and economic gain, especially when it comes to redefining their relations with the US, the world's sole remaining superpower. Through opportunistic readjustments, some states have come out winners in the game, rendering the terrorist attacks and the Age of Fear as a blessing in disguise.

To some extent, this opportunism is strangely reassuring. It ensures that September 11 will not usher in a clash of civilizations. States will always act as states first, mindful of their interests and principles, rather than being driven by primordial instincts and identities. But this is offset by dangers, such as the absence of a genuine commitment to multilateral principles. The fear of transnational terrorism cannot be overcome without resort to significant and genuine multilateral cooperation. International cooperation against terrorism is increasing, both globally and regionally. But there remain many barriers to meaningful cooperation, chief among them the lack of a common understanding of the sources and scope of terror and the continuing salience of national interests over common interest. Changes to the US global strategic doctrine, the pitfalls of an excessively strategic approach to terrorism as may be found in its "re-engagement" in theatres such as Southeast Asia, and the war on Iraq, have accorded little place to multilateralism, yet the latter may hold the key to the legitimacy of a US-led campaign against the fear created by terrorism.

The world's cultural diversity does not necessarily portend a clash of civilizations. Nor does it preclude meaningful cooperation among nations spurred by the common fear of terrorism. But cooperation cannot be bought by American aid nor brought about by the raw exercise of American power, as demonstrated first in Afghanistan and later in Iraq. It will depend upon the development of new norms and principles of conduct to collectively de-legitimize terrorism and sanction principled multilateral intervention without pandering to American hegemony or suppressing our aspirations for freedom and normal living. Otherwise, we are condemned to live indefinitely in the Age of Fear.

Sources

CNN News, May 30, 2003.

David Betz, "Winning the War Mirage: how the coalition did it", *IDSS Commentaries*, May 23, 2003.

Defense News, February 22–23, 2004 (Special Asia Pacific Security Conference Executive News Summary).

Francis Fukuyama, *The End of History and The Last Man* (London: Penguin Books, 1992).

George Yeo, speech prepared for the SIBOS 2001 conference, Ministry of Trade and Industry, Singapore, October 15, 2001.

Irish Times, June 4, 2003.

San Francisco Chronicle, February 9, 2004.

The Economist, November 1, 2003.

2

Who Is a Terrorist?

George Bush is the "king of terrorists", thus spake the Vice President of Indonesia, Hamzah Haz, on April 4, 2003. This was his way of objecting to Bush's use of force to drive Saddam out of Baghdad.

As far as Bush is concerned, going by his official justification of the current war on Iraq, the "Butcher of Baghdad" could well be the "mother of all terrorist regimes".

Malaysia's long-serving prime minister, Mahathir Mohammad, had another favourite target: the state of Israel, America's chief Middle East ally. In his view, Israeli "state terrorism" presents a bigger danger to world peace than terrorist acts by groups or individuals.

The Chinese government has its own take on who are to be called terrorists. On September 18, 2001, a Chinese Foreign Ministry spokesman, commenting on China's reaction to the terrorist attacks on the World Trade Center and the Pentagon, argued: "The United States asks for China's support and assistance in the fight against terrorism. China, in the same token, has reason to ask the United States to give its understanding and support in China's fight against national splittism and terrorism".

Around that time, an unnamed official in Beijing told CNN: "in return for China's contribution to the largely US-led global anti-terrorist crusade, Beijing hoped the US could accommodate Chinese sensitivities in the areas of Taiwan, Xinjiang, Tibet".

These "sensitivities" are usually lumped together under one label: "terrorism, separatism and extremism". The credit for this creative jugglery belongs in the Shanghai Six, a grouping promoted by China as part of its regional security posture towards its western and southwestern neighbours, which under its official name, the Shanghai Cooperation Organisation (SCO), represents the world's first regional anti-terror multilateral coalition. In it, terrorism is defined in terms of its association with separatism and extremism (including political extremism?)

The Russians have not exactly been unwilling partners in this game. In the fall of 2002, Vladimir Putin, President of the Russian

Federation, made an official visit to India and China to explore the possibility of three-way cooperation to challenge the American-dominated "unipolar" world order. Commenting on the discussions and statements issued in Delhi and Beijing, Stanislav Menshikov, a columnist for the *Moscow Tribune*, observed: "The joint statements made in Beijing and Delhi on terrorism have one common feature that differs from the way the term is used in the West. In these new declarations, terrorism is always combined with separatism and extremism. Its meaning is thus broadened to include Chechnya in Russia, Muslim separatism in western China, and the Kashmir issue in India. Russia has reiterated its support for China's sovereignty over Taiwan and Tibet".

Which brings us to the old, tired but not retired, cliché: "One man's terrorist is another man's freedom fighter". It does not stretch the imagination to see that not all terrorists are in the business of "self-determination". For example, Osama's followers in Southeast Asia, the Jemaah Islamiah members, are not "splittists" in the sense that the Chinese government uses the term. They would rather obliterate the nation state framework entirely and replace it with an Islamic superstate.

But there do exist groups which seek nation-state status through self-determination and are willing to engage in means that has been called terrorist by the world's media and governments. Should then they not have their due place in any official definition of terrorism?

Not so simple, says the Organization of Islamic Conference (OIC), a group of 57 Muslim states. In 2002, the OIC met in Kuala Lumpur to come to an agreement on the definition of terrorism. The attempt failed, because condemning the act of terrorism without regard to cause would have implicated the Palestinians, who were viewed by Arab members of the OIC as being engaged in a just struggle for national liberation. "We reject any attempt to link terrorism to the struggle of the Palestinian people in the exercise of their inalienable right to establish their independent state," the OIC Foreign Ministers said in a resolution adopted unanimously. They then went on to "unequivocally" condemn acts of international terrorism "in all its forms and manifestations, including state terrorism".

According to the OIC, under international law and the UN charter, "resistance to foreign aggression, struggle against colonial or alien domination and foreign occupation" were legitimate acts for "national liberation and self-determination".

The OIC meeting ended by stressing the need for an "internationally agreed definition of terrorism, which differentiates legitimate struggle from acts of terror".

We are then back to the "one man's terrorist being another's freedom fighter" question. How do we go about finding a definition "which differentiates legitimate struggle from acts of terror"?

What about the UN? The UN has consciously striven to focus on the act of terror, regardless its motivations. Thus, the United Nations Convention on the Suppression of Financing of Terrorism defines terrorism as any "act intended to cause or serious bodily injury to a civilian, or to any other person not taking an active part in the hostilities in a situation of armed conflict, when the purpose of such act, by its nature or context, is to intimidate a population, or to compel a government or an international organization to do or to abstain from doing any act" [Article 2(1)(b)].

But when the chairman of the UN Security Council's Counter-terrorism Committee, British UN Ambassador Jeremy Greenstock, tried to belabour the point by insisting that "what looks, smells and kills like terrorism is terrorism", he offended Noordin Sopiee, a Malaysian think-tank intellectual. Sopiee dubbed it "racist" (presumably because of the word "smell", but also because it implicated his much beloved but hugely smelly durian, Southeast Asia's king of fruits).

African leaders attending the Commonwealth Heads of Government Meeting (CHOGOM) in Australia in 2002 were reportedly upset over US and British attempts to define terrorism in multilateral fora. Theo-Ben Gurirab, Namibia's foreign minister and a leader of the African Union, lamented: "We are part of the international coalition [against terror]", ..."but at the same time we think the very narrow definition of terrorism is built around only enemies of the US and the West". "We are with the United States in that what happened on September 11 was an act of horror and brutal destruction of life. But because it happened in the US, it has come to overshadow all other viewpoints and considerations".

One of the leaders attending the CHOGOM, South Africa's Thabo Mbeki, was indeed once a freedom fighter on the US State Department's terrorist list.

(Speaking of the US State Department, something about its official definition of terrorism did not get through to me. It includes, among other things, the "use of any (a) biological agent, chemical agent, or nuclear weapon or device, or (b) explosive or firearm *(other than for mere personal monetary gain)*, with intent to endanger, directly or indirectly, the safety of one or more individuals or to cause substantial damage to property." (emphasis added). Are we supposed to infer that use of explosives and firearms for "personal monetary gain" are not to be classified as terrorism?)

To be sure, Africans who used to be on the various lists of terrorist groups kept by Western governments did not use tactics that we normally associate with Osama bin Laden. Despite such acts as the blowing up a restaurant in Durban, South Africa, in the mid-1980s, most of the targets of militant African freedom fighters were assets such as electrical transmission lines and bridges, which had military value to the governments they were fighting.

But there is an irony here. Many of the governments protesting the narrow definition that fails to differentiate between terrorists and freedom fighters are themselves likely to press for a wider definition when it comes to dealing with their ethnic minorities. Martin Schonteich, a researcher with the Institute of Security Studies in Pretoria, warns that some African governments may even use the war on terrorism to crack down on their Muslim minorities. "In Uganda, you already have non-Muslims exploiting the war to make accusations against Muslim communities in the hope they will get some aid from the West".

How do we get some "clarity" here? Typing "definition of terrorism" in a Google Internet search, I came up with 286,000 entries. A second search, this time under "terrorism definition" yielded 287,000 entries. Helpless and hopeless, I clicked on the very first entry.

It took me to a website called *The Rational Radical* (http://www.therationalradical.com), which promises to give the reader/browser "a radical alternative view of American politics and culture". Among its gems is a feature called *The Daily Diatribe*. According to this, one should avoid "subjective evaluations of the goals of the violence", and instead focus on the target of violence and the nature of the perpetrator. One should hence distinguish between use of violence "where one would reasonably expect harm to innocent civilians" from "a 'military' action, where the use of violence is not reasonably expected to harm innocent civilians." Similarly, a "state" action (or action by a "sovereign government") should be differentiated from "guerrilla action", (conducted by "a non-governmental entity"). In this way, one could have both state military actions and state terrorist actions. Likewise, there can be both guerrilla military actions and guerrilla terrorist actions.

Going by this formulation, if a country sends its bombers to attack military airfields of its enemy, that would qualify as a state military action. But if a country sends its bombers to destroy the civilian infrastructure of another nation (such as water or power supplies, or telephone exchanges), this would be a state act of terrorism, because harm to civilians would "reasonably" be expected to result. This formulation might please Hamzah Haz (who could point the finger at the water shortages in Basra resulting from US military action), but would not have solved the targeting woes of General Tommy Franks. General Franks' US Central Command was hugely miffed that Iraqi military personnel routinely hide in civilian places.

Similarly, if a group seeking self-determination or some other political objective sends a suicide bomber to blow up a civilian café (or passenger bus, as Palestinian radicals have frequently done to buses loaded with Israeli civilians), this would be a guerrilla act of terrorism. But if it sends a boat-load of explosives to blow up a military vessel, that would be a guerrilla military action. The latter is sure to enrage the Pentagon, which lost the USS Cole in the port of Aden.

Perhaps we can live without a common definition of terrorism? In 1977, Walter Laqueur noted that "the disputes about a detailed, comprehensive definition of terrorism will continue for a long time, they will not result in a consensus and they will make no notable contribution towards the understanding of terrorism".

I ditto that for the next 26 years and beyond.

Appendix

The US State Department's definition of terrorist activity:

TERRORIST ACTIVITY DEFINED—As used in this Act, the term "terrorist activity" means any activity which is unlawful under the laws of the place where it is committed (or which, if committed in the United States, would be unlawful under the laws of the United States or any State) and which involves any of the following:

(I) The hijacking or sabotage of any conveyance (including an aircraft, vessel, or vehicle).

(II) The seizing or detaining, and threatening to kill, injure, or continue to detain, another individual in order compel a third person (including a governmental organization) to do or abstain from doing any act as an explicit or implicit condition for the release of the individual seized or detained.

(III) A violent attack upon an internationally protected person (as defined in section 1116(b)(4) of title 18, United States code) or upon the liberty of such a person.

(IV) An assassination.

(V) The use of any—
  (a) biological agent, chemical agent, or nuclear weapon or device, or
  (b) explosive or firearm (other than for mere personal monetary gain), with intent to endanger, directly or indirectly, the safety of one or more individuals or to cause substantial damage to property.

(VI) A threat, attempt, or conspiracy to do any of the foregoing.

ENGAGE IN TERRORIST ACTIVITY DEFINED—As used in the Act, the term "engage in terrorist activity" means to commit, in an individual capacity or as a member of an organization, an act of terrorist activity or an act which the actor knows, or reasonably should know, affords material support to any individual, organization, or government in conducting a terrorist activity at any time, including any of the following acts:

(I) The preparation or planning of a terrorist activity.

(II) The gathering of information on potential targets for terrorist activity.

(III) The providing of any type of material support, including a safe house, transportation, communication, funds, false identification, weapons, explosives, or training, to any individual the actor knows or has reason to believe has committed or plans to commit a terrorist activity.

(IV) The soliciting of funds or other things of value for terrorist activity of for any terrorist organization.

(V) The solicitation of any individual for membership in a terrorist organization, terrorist government, or to engage in a terrorist activity.

(From Section 212 (a)(3)(B) of the Immigration and Nationality Act)

Sources

BBC Monitoring International Reports, April 2, 2002.

Moscow Tribune, December 6, 2002.

M2 Presswire, April 8, 2002; *Christian Science Monitor*, March 20, 2002.

Sopiee, Noordin, "What Is Terrorism? Who is a Terrorist? Why Terrorism?", Paper presented at the 16th Asia Pacific Roundtable, Kuala Lumpur, June 2–5, 2002. *Japan Economic Newswire*, April 2, 2002.

The Daily Diatribe: a radical alternative view of American politics and culture, at http://www.therationalradical.com/.

World News Connection, April 2, 2003.

Culture, Fear and the Roots of Terror

Fear n.

1. *a. A feeling of agitation and anxiety caused by the presence or imminence of danger.*
   b. A state or condition marked by this feeling: living in fear.
2. *A feeling of disquiet or apprehension:* a fear of looking foolish.
3. *Extreme reverence or awe, as toward a supreme power.*
4. *A reason for dread or apprehension:* Being alone is my greatest fear.

   http://dictionary.reference.com/search?q=fear

Terrorism: "the calculated use of violence or the threat of violence to inculcate fear; intended to coerce or to intimidate governments or societies in the pursuit of goals that are generally political, religious, or ideological."
US Department of Defense,
http://www.globalterrorism101.com/UTDefinition.html

Fear is evil, without evil there would be no fear … Fear is the opposite of life, hope, joy, peace and love. Fear is man's worst enemy and a terrorist's best tool.
Christopher K. 8th Grade From "Peace Roots" (Published by KIDS FOR PEACE. www.kidsforpeace.org)

3

Clash of Civilizations? No, of National Interests and Principles

The swift collapse of the Taliban regime in Afghanistan under the weight of American military power marks the defeat of one of the more prominent ideas to emerge from the ashes of the Cold War: Samuel Huntington's thesis about a "clash of civilizations". The September 11 attacks on the United States were the first real test of the Huntington thesis. Amid the initial shock waves of the attacks, many saw its vindication. This view gained strength when George W. Bush used the world "crusade", with its connotations of a Christian holy war against Muslims. The attacks themselves were presented by the perpetrators as Islamic holy war against Christians and Jews. Yet the response of governments and peoples around the world has proved that this was no clash of civilizations. What emerged was an old-fashioned struggle over the interests and principles that have traditionally governed international relations. Civilizational affinities played only a secondary role. The world's Muslim nations condemned the terrorist attacks. Many recognized the US' right to retaliate against the Taliban for sheltering Al-Qaeda. Some offered material and logistical assistance. From Saudi Arabia to Pakistan, from Iran to Indonesia, Islamic nations denounced bin Laden.

In Pakistan, President Pervez Musharraf and his associates denounced the terrorists for giving Islam a bad name. Reversing its long sponsorship of the Taliban and braving the wrath of Islamic extremists at home, Pakistan offered vital logistical support to US forces. Iran, which for decades had spearheaded Islamic revolutionaries' campaigns against the United States, also made no secret of its disdain for the Taliban's Islamic credentials. Iran saw an opportunity to rid itself of an unfriendly regime in its neighbourhood. Each of these nations put national interest and modern principles of international conduct above primordial sentiment and transnational religious or cultural identity. Pakistan, for example, got badly needed American aid and de facto recognition of its military regime.

Indonesia, whose support as the world's most populous Islamic nation was crucial to the legitimacy of the US-led anti-terrorist campaign, received American economic and political backing for its fledgling democracy. In Indonesia and Malaysia, the war against terrorism presented an opportunity for governments to rein in domestic Islamic extremists who had challenged their authority and created public disorder.

Most nations accepted the US counterstrike as an exercise in a nation's right of self-defence. None granted the same right to the Taliban.

Asked to choose between America and the terrorists, nations of the world closed ranks to an unprecedented degree and sided against the terrorists. They did so despite reservations about America's Middle East policy, concerns about civilian casualties in the Afghanistan war and misgivings about US military and economic dominance of the world.

The "clash of civilizations" thesis fares no better in the domestic arena than on the international stage. Appalled by the terrorists' methods and the loss of so many innocent lives, most religious leaders in Islamic societies condemned the attacks as un-Islamic.

Dire predictions were made that countries which acquiesced in or backed the US retaliation would be torn apart by ethnic and religious strife, but such predictions did not come true. In Pakistan, where the risk was most serious, General Musharraf was able to act more and more boldly against extremists as Islamic protests fizzled out. Hard-core Islamic elements in Indonesia failed in their attempt to rally widespread public support against the American action in Afghanistan. In Malaysia, Prime Minister Mahathir bin Mohamad set aside his rhetoric against American hegemony and made it difficult for Malaysian jihadists to travel to Afghanistan to fight alongside the Taliban. The international response to the September 11 terrorist attacks shows that religion and civilization do not replace pragmatism, interest and principle as the guiding motives of international relations. In rejecting the call to jihad issued by the Taliban, Osama bin Laden and their supporters, some Islamic nations acted out of interest and others out of principle. Most were motivated by a combination of both.

Sources

Huntington, Samuel, *The Clash of Civilizations and the Revoking of World Order*, New York: Touchstone Books, 1997.

4

Hatred, Harmony and the Causes of Terror

What causes terrorism? A fundamental basis of civilizational identity, religion has been implicated in most violent conflicts in history and in almost all cases of genocide in the 20th century. At a forum entitled Asia Vision 21, organised by the Harvard University's Asia Center in 2002, one speaker—a Harvard professor—argued that the secular nation state is a fairly recent phenomenon in history, but the link between religion and politics long predates it. Nationalists have frequently used religion and ethnicity for political ends, despite professing a secular ideology. Religion can be used for political ends in a variety of ways. One recent example which associates religion with terrorism is US President George W. Bush's use of Christian rhetoric, including a reference to the crusades, to justify revenge after the September 11 terrorist attacks on the US.

Huntington's "clash of civilizations" thesis has the virtue of recognizing the role of religion and culture as forces for conflict. The notion that global secular modernity constitutes an end point of modernization is flawed. The world is not moving in that direction. Religion remains a basis of nation-state. The Harvard professor insisted that the view of the world experiencing a retreat from religion as a social and political force is antiquated. On the contrary, religion and ethnicity are reasserting themselves. Linguistic identity is not disappearing. One main reason for this trend is a dramatic demographic shift from the Christian West to Africa, Asia and Latin America. This trend is reflected in the growing Muslim population, and the rise of Islamic revivalism. We also see trends towards Buddhist renewal in East Asia and Hindu self-assertion in India. We see many cases of ethnic hatred and conflict, ranging from the Tamils in Sri Lanka, to the Hutus and Tutsis in Central Africa, to the ethnic sectarian strife in Northern Ireland.

But do these trends make a clash of civilizations inevitable? Religion is a factor in conflict, but there are good reasons to view it not as the direct cause, but rather as a catalyst. The local/regional interplay between religion and ethnic identity in many parts of the world makes religious identity a rallying point for politics and a possible fuel for revolutionary conflict. But religion and ethnicity have not, and will not displace nationalism, which remains essentially a political force.

The point was brought home by a Bangladeshi delegate to the Asia Vision 21 forum, who noted the presence of 450 million Muslims in the Indian subcontinent. What would have been the situation if there had there been no partition of India by the British? If the British had given the people of East Bengal a choice between an independent Bengal and Pakistan, they would have mostly likely opted for independence. To the delegate, this showed that nationalism is more important than religion.

If nationalism can undermine intra-civilizational solidarity, economics can bridge inter-civilizational faultlines. Southeast Asia sets an example of why the fact of multi-ethnicity need not spell doom for inter-civilizational harmony if the economics are sound. As a Southeast Asian speaker at the same forum claimed, it is in Malaysia that Southeast Asia offers the most economically successful Muslim nation in the world, the "model of a modern, economic successful and tolerant Islamic nation", although this phenomenon might have been obscured by Dr Mahathir's outspokenness. Malaysia has transformed itself from a colonial plantation economy to a modern industrial economy. "When Mahathir came to power, the primary sector accounted for 80% of the GDP, now, the industrial sector produces 80% of the GDP". It escaped the kind of ethnic strife that followed the 1997 economic crisis in Indonesia. Another Malaysian delegate supported this view by pointing out that the number of Hindu temples in Malaysia reportedly exceeds the total number of Hindu temples in Tamil Nadu, India. And for him, the 1969 ethnic riots in Malaysia were over economic and not religious issues.

But economic development in the absence of equity does not blunt, and may even fuel, inter-civilizational mistrust. Indonesia is the world's most populous Muslim nation. The Indonesian experience shows that development does not necessarily lead to secularization. This desire for modernization without Westernisation is due to the West's link with colonialism. The rise of Islamic forces in Indonesia was partly a reaction against the authoritarian policies of the Suharto government. The anti-state movement against Suharto drew sustenance from religion, a kind of Muslim liberation theology. But greater mobilization of Islam does not translate into increased political power. Dozens of Islamic political parties which rose after the downfall of Suharto did not see political success. Islamic groups in Indonesia are too divided to constitute a potent political force.

There are other examples showing why the influence of Islam on Indonesian politics could be overstated. The 1998 anti-Chinese riots in Indonesia were due to economic, and not religious divisions. The ethnic riots in Ambon today are also about power, not religion *per se*. Islam is often used in an instrumental way in many cases of conflict in Indonesia. For example, some Muslim politicians in Indonesia tried to prevent Megawati Sukarnoputri from being elected president because Islam supposedly forbade a woman from being president. But the very same people supported her when she helped to impeach and remove the then incumbent president of the country, Abdurrahaman Wahid, who had for a long time headed the largest Islamic organization in Indonesia.

If religion is important, it may only be as a scapegoat for other root causes such as the demand for equality. Most conflicts in the world today are domestic in nature. And many are rooted in poverty, food scarcity, population growth and other problems of globalization, religion and ethnicity. A good deal of the debate over the so-called "root causes" of terror would pit poverty against politics as its fundamental underlying cause. Most participants at the Harvard forum would dismiss as a "cliché" that poverty and economic underdevelopment fuels militant Islam. As one Southeast Asian businessman at the Harvard forum put it, these are convenient excuses for getting aid from the US. There is no direct link between poverty and terror. Kuwait is an example of how a rich country can face the danger of militant Islam. In India, the state of Gujarat is one of the most prosperous parts of India, yet it has been recently torn by inter-religious violence. Many argue that poverty represents a security problem, but some of the poorest countries are the most peaceful while some of the most affluent countries are home to terrorists, claimed this participant.

It may be more useful to bring poverty into the picture in another way. Proponents of terror, Muslim or otherwise, are not themselves poverty-stricken people, but professionals who are *concerned* with the issue of poverty and injustice. The anger of the September 11 terrorists was directed against their own governments as much as against the US. Some gospel interpretations of Islam focus on injustice and societal unfairness. Terrorists and leaders of fundamentalist movements are often concerned with the fairness or lack thereof in their own societies. Thus, the perception of fairness/unfairness is as important as religion and economics as causes of conflict and terrorism.

Add humiliation to unfairness. Books written by Osama bin-Laden make frequent references to humiliation. A Korean participant at the forum cautioned against using humiliation as a category since countries and groups can be mistakenly accused of inflicting humiliation on minorities or other religions even when there was no such intention on their part. But humiliation does play its part. Colonial imperial history, with their narratives of contempt and humiliation, continue to be important factors behind conflict. The Arab-Israeli conflict, for example, is not so much about religion, but about Israel as a colonial presence in the Middle East and seen as an extension of the US and Europe in the region. Solving religious and ethnic conflict depends on justice and fairness from outside and moderate voices from inside.

Perhaps the most powerful argument against the clash of civilizations thesis is the heterogeneity of Islam. As does Christianity, Islam has many branches and sects. Islam in the Middle East is different from Islam in the subcontinent. There are variations within Islam in the subcontinent as well. Islamic fundamentalists who have tried to capitalize on religion for electoral purposes have largely failed. In Bangladesh, Islamic political parties have never captured more than 8 per cent of the vote. Hence, a delegate from Malaysia cautioned against interpreting recent developments in religious terms. To him, September 11 is not a Muslim or religious problem. The September 11 terrorists were irreligious. Rather, Southeast Asians would dismiss September 11 as a Middle East problem.

September 11 is also a political problem. As an Indian-born American professor put it, in the Middle East, the main factors in conflict are not religious, but political, and linked to injustice.

Moreover, one has to deconstruct religion as a category. Religious sensitivity is different from religious bigotry, which in turn is different from religious majoritarianism. Religious majoritarianism, a by-product of democratic politics, lies at the heart of recent religious riots in India's Gujarat.

Most religious conflicts boil down to a fight for political space and legitimacy. Most cases of fundamentalism arise when newly affluent classes take religion as a form of self-assertion. Fundamentalism is thus a middle class phenomenon, and should not be explained as a by-product of poverty.

For another Indian participant in the forum, the key to understanding terrorism is personality cults, rather than politics or religion *per se*. Terror grows around personalities. In India, Sikh terrorism in the 1980s grew around the personality of Jarnail Singh Bhindranwale. His killing by Indian security forces did not lead to more uprisings of Sikhs; instead Sikh terrorism disappeared. In Sri Lanka, the Tamil Tigers are not driven by religious or political impetus, but by the personality cult around their leader Prabhakaran. Thus, economic, political and even ethnic factors are less important than personality. Bin Laden's case is the same. Commenting on the perception that "all Muslims are not terrorists, but all terrorists are Muslims", Gupta pointed out that most terrorists groups today are not pan-national, but those few which are, tend to be Muslim.

How to overcome terrorism? For one Malaysian participant, pragmatism and accommodation are two key principles behind Malaysia's success in maintaining ethnic harmony. Turning to September 11, he argued that the factors that led to these terrorist attacks on the US were not religious. Rather, many people felt that "they could not share" in America's wealth or standard of living. America must recognize this feeling, otherwise there will be no harmony.

For another participant the search for moderate Muslims as an answer to September 11 is better abandoned. It might lead to oppressive regimes receiving support, as happened after September 11. In fact the very notion of "moderate Muslim" implies that Islam is normally extremist. The idea of a moderate Muslim may have a positive connotation in the West, but not in Muslim societies.

The forum concluded with the view that conflicts today should not be viewed as being over culture, religion or civilization, but as political and economic conflicts that arise as societies cope with globalization. A common theme that emerged was that the importance of religion and ethnicity as root causes of conflict and terrorism today could be overstated. Similarly, poverty and underdevelopment are not necessarily the main or most important factors behind terrorism and conflict. Religion is often used in an instrumental way in conflicts. Many religious conflicts and instances of terrorism today are political contestations for power and legitimacy which take the guise of religion and ethnicity. While ethnic and religious forces behind conflict are not to be disregarded, other factors should be taken into account, such as the role of humiliation, colonial memories and developments of personality cults, the latter especially in terrorist movements. The clash of civilizations thesis is flamed and limited to the extent that politics and the associated struggle for power and legitimacy, lie at the heart of many conflicts which take on the appearance of a clash of civilizations. The Muslim world is not monolithic. Nor is it uniformly inward-looking. Southeast Asia in general and Malaysia in particular offer important examples of religious tolerance and economic and political modernity in the Muslim world.

5

The Fear of Islam

President George W. Bush responded to the September 11 attacks by likening America's war on terror to a "crusade". The remark was branded an unfortunate slip-up and the media was blamed for distorting it. But Franklin Graham—son of Billy Graham, America's most famous evangelist, who gave the prayer at W's inaugural—told NBC News after September 11: "It wasn't Methodists flying into those buildings, and it wasn't Lutherans. It was an attack on this country by people of the Islamic faith". For Graham, Islam is a "very wicked and evil" religion. After the US victory in Iraq, he was invited by the Pentagon to deliver its Good Friday service.

In such minds, the fear of terrorism equates fear (and loathing) of Islam. There is something about Islam that lends itself to terrorism. No one articulates this more clearly than the Reverend Ted Haggard, president of the National Association of Evangelicals. He was responding to Bush in his November 2003 news conference in London when he stated that Christians and Muslims worship the same god. What Bush had said is this: "I do say that freedom is the Almighty's gift to every person. I also condition it by saying freedom is not America's gift to the world. It's much greater than that, of course. And I believe we worship the same god." According to Haggard, the Christian and Muslim Gods could not be more different:

> The Christian God encourages freedom, love, forgiveness, prosperity and health. The Muslim god appears to value the opposite. The personalities of each god are evident in the cultures, civilizations and dispositions of the peoples that serve them. Muhammad's central mission was submission; Jesus' central message was love. They seem to be very different personalities.

Such culturalist views of Islam may be one reason why the "clash of civilizations" thesis refuses to die away. Yet, the fear of Islam distorts the understanding of terrorism as a rational and political instrument.

Singapore's Senior Minister, Lee Kuan Yew, recognizes the political underpinnings of contemporary terrorism, although he considers it irrational. "It was a bid for power", read the title of an interview he gave to the *Straits Times* on the Jemaah Islamiah arrests in Singapore in December 2001. According to Lee, "It's a bid for power. They want to create a Muslim state, or Daulah Islamiyah, a caliphate that comprises Malaysia, Indonesia, south Philippines and Singapore. It's absurd, not achievable. Suppose they were to gain power as the communists did in Eastern Europe, did they become one great communist state? Why should Thai, Malaysian or Filipino Muslims give up power and surrender sovereignty to this caliphate led by Indonesians? But in the struggle for power, it's a tremendous inspirational pull: 'We are the purest, we fight for God'".

Robert Pape, Professor of Political Science at the University of Chicago argues that suicide terrorism, the most fearsome form of modern terrorism, is a strategic (hence rational) weapon employed by terrorists to coerce and intimidate democracies, Pape offers a new account of why there has been an escalation of the use of suicide terrorism as a tactic in places such as Sri Lanka from 1990, Lebanon in 1985, Turkey in the late 1990s, and the Gaza Strip and West Bank in 1994 and 1995. Ideological propensities, psychological bases and socio-economic backgrounds do not provide satisfactory explanations. By tracking suicide terrorist attacks from 1980 to 2001, Pape's conclusion is that suicide terrorism follows a strategic logic. The effectiveness in coercing modern liberal democracies into making substantial territorial compromises renders suicide terrorism widespread. Terrorist groups that employ such tactics enjoy gains that add more fuel to their political cause. The implications this has for democracies is a policy shift from offensive military action to improving homeland security and this shift will drive home the lesson that gains from suicide terrorism are no longer possible.

Returning to the link between Islam and terrorism, findings by Professor Ariel Merari of Tel Aviv University are particularly instructive.[1] His studies show that religious fanaticism is not the main cause of suicide terrorism, secular Arab Bathists and Kurdish Marxists have carried out suicide attacks. About two-thirds of the suicide attacks in Lebanon were carried out by secular groups. Moreover, Islam hardly has the monopoly over suicide terrorism; Lebanese Christians, Hindu and Christian Tamils have had their share of such attacks. Hence, religious fanaticism, Islamic or other types, is neither a necessary nor a sufficient factor behind suicide terrorism. Merari also rejects poverty (the Saudi perpetrators of 9/11), ignorance (the educated Palestinian bomber), psychopathology (in his view, few of the suicide bombers in Israel would be hospitalised by the district psychologist) as factors behind suicide attacks. Instead, he blames such attacks on group pressure and organizational manipulation (not a single attacker he studied did it on his or her own will; an organization was always involved).

Can terrorism be regarded as a form of collective resistance strategy? The argument may run like this. The West defeated and colonized the Islamic World. Islam lost its scientific edge. Islam has become humiliated. But Islamic nations cannot hit back at the West. They can fight one another, but not their conquerors and tormentors. To add salt to the wound is the occupation of Palestine. Mahathir Mohamad, the then Prime Minister of Malaysia, spoke of humiliation at least five times in his speech at the opening of the Tenth Session of the Islamic Summit Conference in Malaysia on October 16, 2003. Thomas Friedman, a journalist who has won a Pulitzer Prize for his coverage of the Middle East, calls humiliation the most underrated force in international relations. Hence Islam turns to terrorism. Terrorism is easier to organize and direct. Terrorism requires no big guns, no stealth technology, no vast standing armies, no fighting jets. Terrorism uses civilian jets and turns them into mini atomic weapons. Terrorists can take advantage of globalization, and the low cost of free technology like the internet. No surprise then that the Internet is the single most important tool of Al-Qaeda. Terrorism is insidious. It hides well. Terrorists take advantage of visa-free travel and porous borders. The reason why Southeast Asia has become the second front of terrorism is because Taliban alumni and Middle Eastern terrorists have made a rational calculation. The Middle East/Gulf states are especially inhospitable—internal secret acts are too harsh, repression too strong. Hence they migrated to Southeast Asia where travel is risk-free, people are friendly and multicultural, governments are corrupt, and globalization is rampant, not to mention there are ongoing internal conflicts to take advantage of. Hence, Southeast Asia is terrorism's rational frontier.

But shared humiliation and backwardness do not make for a monolithic group. Singaporean academic Syed Farid Alatas[2] argues that while there is a link between Islam and terrorism, a distinction must be made between "Islamic extremism" and "Muslim extremism". The former implicates the whole of the religion. The latter is more selective and discriminating. From the Muslim point of view, the Islamic extremism is a contradiction because Islam defines itself as a religion of the middle way. Alatas also makes a distinction between the two types of orientation in Islam: ideology and utopia. As ideology, Islam legitimises an existing order (as in the case of Wahabism in Saudhi Arabia). As utopia, islam challenges an existing order, often using terror as a means (as in the case of parts of Southeast Asia). Hence, the perception of Islam as a religion of extremists bent on disrupting the status quo is unjustified.

There is plenty of diversity within Islam. The two major "Islamic terrorist" organizations in Southeast Asia, the JI and MILF, have different conceptions of Islamic statehood. The former believes in a supranational state, the latter sticks to the old-fashioned nation-state framework. French scholar Amélie Blom[3] who has closely studied jihadi networks in Pakistan argues that "there is not a typical sociological profile of the candidates to martyrdom." Some jihadi are "playful", seeking bragging rights and glory through terrorist attacks, while other may be tempted by material gain, while still others are "martyropaths", (as in psychopaths).

Islam has no coherent body of doctrine that legitimizes (or de-legitimizes) terrorism. Rather, the impulse to terrorism extremism may depends on how Islam is taught. Hence the most potent weapon against Muslim terror is education.

Even if we are to draw a link between terror and Islam, the link is forged by historical context, socio-economic conditions and political and strategic calculations. It is not rooted in some innate or primordial characteristics of Islam. If we recognise the diversity within Islam and if we recognise terrorism as a strategic weapon of the weak, then we have a better chance of fighting it rather than turning the fear of Islam into a self-fulfilling prophecy.

Endnotes

1 Ariel Merari, Presentation to the "Joint seminar on Terrorism: The Singaporean and Israeli Experience," April 12–13, 2004, Singapore.

2 Syed Farid Alatas, Presentation on "Islam and the Nation State", at the second France-Singapore Conference, co-organized by the Institute of Defence and Strategic Studies (Singapore) and Centre asie ifri (Paris), November 10–11, 2003, Singapore

3 Amélie Blom, "The Dynamics of Martydom and Jihadist Networks: Southeast Asia France-Singapore Conference, co-organized by the Insistute of Defence and Strategic Studies (Singapore) and Centre asie ifri (Paris), November 10–11, 2003, Singapore.

Sources

AFX-Asia, December 6, 2002.

Amélie Blom, *Straits Times*, December 6, 2002.

New York Times, 22 April 2003.

Robert A. Pape, "The Strategic Logic of Suicide Terrorism", *American Political Science Review* Vol. 97, No. 3 (August 2003).

Syed Farid Alatas, "Islam and Modernization", in Conference on "Islam in South East Asia: Political, Social and Strategic Challenges for the 21st Century", Singapore, Institute of Southeast Asian Studies, September 2–3, 2002.

Washington Post, November 22, 2003.

6

Terror in Southeast Asia: Local or Global?

Since September 11, 2001, Southeast Asia has been termed by the US as the "second front" in the global war on terror. This view rests on the belief that with its defeat in Afghanistan, Al-Qaeda elements shifted their attention to Southeast Asia. Southeast Asians who trained in Afghanistan returned home where they could respond to the Al-Qaeda leadership's periodic call for terrorist strikes (both low- and high-impact) Southeast Asia offered an attractive home to international terrorism, thanks to a combination of factors. Firstly, its multi-ethnic societies. Secondly, its weak and corrupt regimes with a tenuous hold over peripheral areas. Thirdly, its ongoing separatist insurgencies that lend themselves to exploitation by foreign elements. Moreover in some cases undergoing painful democratic transactions, governments, weakened by the financial crisis; as in Indonesia and the Philippines, could not mobilize public support for security regulations to ensure preventive suppression of terrorist elements.

A terrorist plot aimed at Singapore was uncovered in December 2001. The plot specifically targeted US military installations and the personnel stationed there, underscoring the intra-regional dimension of the challenge. The suspected perpetrators of the planned attacks are believed to be members of the Jemaah Islamiah (JI) organization, whose objectives include the creation of a pan-Southeast Asian Islamic state comprising the Muslim-majority areas of southern Philippines, Indonesia, Malaysia, Singapore and southern Thailand. The combination of the pan-regional blueprint and the transregional training and support network of its adherents has contributed to the perception of an even larger threat to Southeast Asian security that transcends local or national grievances and faultlines.

Is Southeast Asia really the second front for global terrorism? Or is terrorism locally produced, reflecting conflicts and injustices which would exist even without external aid? Some scholars, such as Rohan Gunaratna, see Southeast Asian terrorism as being intimately linked to the global transnational network, Al-Qaeda, which orchestrates, however loosely, the training, financing and even operational leadership of local incidents such as the attack on Bali. Terrorists are like sharks, looking for fresh opportunities to exploit. Thus, when the Taliban was driven out of Afghanistan and Middle Eastern governments tightened their control, terrorists found Southeast Asia, with its relatively open societies, corrupt regimes and multi-ethnic settings, a convenient destination to move into.

A second school of thought, led by scholars like Farish Noor of Malaysia, rejects this view as being unduly alarmist and based on a superficial understanding of the sources of conflict and violence in the region. It argues that terrorism is based essentially on local sources, such as poverty, maldistribution of wealth and lack of democracy.

In reality, both views are half right. When we look at the Bali bombings of October 12, 2002, clear evidence has emerged that the perpetrators received aid and advice from Al-Qaeda. But most forms of terrorism in Southeast Asia are local. Without local grievances and the weaknesses of local institutions, terrorism will not thrive. Moreover, the motivations behind terrorism can vary, from country to country, or region to region within the same country, or from time to time.

A report published in December 2002 by the Brussels-based International Crisis Group offers an interesting window on the varied and changing motivations of terrorists groups within Indonesia itself. The report notes that the conflicts in Maluku and Poso were an integral component of JI's recruitment and development of combat and military skills. These two Indonesian foci could eclipse Afghanistan and the southern Philippines as training centres. How far the arm of recruitment can reach has implications not only for preparing Indonesian Islamic radicals, but for the entire JI network. Maluku and Poso rose in significance because these were the sites of communal conflict that inspired the vengeful Bali attack. Videos about the massacres in the Indonesian hotspots often prefaced the recruitment of foot soldiers. Those bloodbaths served the twin functions of lending a more concrete understanding to the concept of jihad (a central pillar of JI's ideology) and furnishing readily available locations for training of recruits.

There are important variations in the nature and objectives of terrorist groups in Southeast Asia. First, there are those seeking to punish rival ethnic groups in a situation of ethnic hatred and conflict, as is the case with some anti-Christian radical groups in Indonesia. The second is a more common type comprising those seeking independence or autonomy from post-colonial nation-states. These are classical separatist movements who are now branded as terrorist groups by governments and analysts partly with a view to delegitimize them. These movements feed hatred for the ruling regime dominated by a rival ethnic group, which is seen as persecuting the minority group. Examples of this type include the MILF and the Abu Sayyaf in outhern Philippines. Finally, some terrorist groups are seeking to establish a pan-Islamic state. They are motivated by a religious fervour as well as dislike of the existing regimes, especially their pro-Western orientation. The best example of this is the Jemaah Islamiah group in Southeast Asia.

Despite these differences, some officials in Southeast Asia see no reason to avoid implicating radical Islam as the important common element binding these groups. As a senior Singapore official, Eddie Teo puts it:

> It may not be politically correct to focus on the relationship between Islam and terrorism. However, the common thread that seemed to unite JI members was their desire for spiritual revival ... What they were ... taught was that to be a good, genuine Muslim, you would have to hate the West, bring down secular, pro-Western governments in the region and pave the way for an Islamic regional government.

Despite having emerged under different circumstances, several terrorist groups in Southeast Asia have joined together for strategic and tactical reasons, including the need for financial and logistics support, training facilities and protection against state security officials. The Jemmal Islamial is the most important regional terror network in Southeast Asia with its existence highlighted by the discovery in December 2001 of a terrorist plot in Singapore targeted specifically at the US military installations and personnel stationed there. The JI's objective includes the creation of a pan-Southeast Asian Islamic state comprising the southern Philippines, Indonesia,

Malaysia, Singapore and southern Thailand (Australia is also part of its territorial organization). The combination of the pan-regional blueprint and the transregional training and support network of its adherents has contributed to the perception of an even larger threat to Southeast Asian security, transcending local or national grievances and faultlines. To further its regional networking, the JI set up the Rabitatul Mujahidin, a regional caucus of leaders of various Southeast Asian terror organizations—comprising JI and representatives from MILF, groups in Aceh, Rohingyas of Myanmar, and Sulawesi, as well as an unnamed group from southern Thailand—so that the "groups could co-operate and share resources for training, procurement of arms, financial assistance and terrorist operations".

According to a Singapore White Paper on the terrorist network, JI "is the group which enjoys the closest relationship with the Al-Qaeda organization in the region." JI recruits trained with the Al-Qaeda in Afghanistan from the 1990s. And it was Al-Qaeda which supported Singaporean members of the JI planning attacks against US targets in Singapore. At the destroyed home of a senior Al-Qaeda leader, Mohamed Atef, in Afghanistan the tapes of JI's planned attacks in Singapore were found, which then led to the eventual arrest of the network members in Singapore.

Terrorism in Southeast Asian is thus neither exclusively global nor exclusively local. It's both. It breeds from local causes, but draws sustenance from the outside. Issues like the Palestine question and resentment against the global dominance of the US give legitimacy to terrorist causes. Although many terrorist groups have religious roots, their motivations are ultimately political, the chief aim being to seize power in their respective states or in the region. Ultimately therefore, the challenge of terrorism in Southeast Asia is both a challenge to regime security as well as the nation-state system comprising post-colonial boundaries.

Sources

Alameda Times-Star, December 5, 2002.

Associated Press, International News, December 11, 2002.

Eddie Teo (Permanent Secretary, Prime Minister's Office), "Jemaah Islamiyah: Answering the Question: Why", Talks at Brookings Institution, November 25, 2002.

Farish A. Noor, "Demonisation of Innocent Islamic Groups", *Straits Times*, October 30, 2002.

Indonesia Backgrounder: How the Jemaah Islamiyah Terrorist Group Operates, Asia Report No. 43 (Jakarta: International Crisis Group, December 11, 2002).

Ministry of Home Affairs, Singapore, *The Jemmah Islamiyah Arrests and the Threat of Terrorism*, White Paper 2003.

Rohan Gunaratna, "Gravity of Terrorism Shifting to Region", *Straits Times*, October 15, 2002.

The Cairns Post, October 14, 2002.

Xinhua News Agency (General News) January 10, 2003.

7

Pakistan: Riding the Terrorist Tiger

The story begins with the Soviet occupation of Afghanistan between 1979 and 1988. An ally of the US in the Cold War divide, Pakistan became the nerve centre for planning, coordination training and execution of an anti-Soviet jihad for which many Muslims from the Arab world and Southeast Asia, the Chechens, the Egyptians, the Yemenies as well as volunteered to assist. In 1984, Abdullah Azzam, a Palestinian scholar and former leader of the Muslim Brotherhood Organisation (Al-Iqwanul Muslamoon) and Osama bin Laden cofounded the Maktab al Khidamat lil Mujahidin al-Arab-MAK, (or Afghan Service Bureau) in Peshawar, Pakistan as a forum to disseminate propaganda, raise funds and recruit mujahideens. The MAK set up a network of offices in 35 countries (including 30 in US cities). The bureau received substantial official patronage from Islamabad and Washington in terms of armaments, experts for training, intelligence support and networking. In 1988, Azam and Osama bin Laden set up Al-Qaeda al-Sulbah (The Solid Base) to create a worldwide framework of Islamist military and political organizations. After Azzam's death, Osama turned MAK, together with Al-Qaeda, into a global terrorist front.

The transmigration of terrorists and the infrastructure was of such magnitude that many intelligence analysts believed that the centre of gravity of terrorism had shifted from the Middle East to Asia. This shift manifested itself principally in two forms. Afghanistan replaced Lebanon as the major centre for terrorist training and infrastructure. Second, the agenda of jihad was widened, to include local conflicts, making these part of an international Islamic jihad. In effect, Afghanistan emerged as the headquarters of international terrorism. This was due mainly to facilitation by a regime that had no difficulty in identifying state interests with those of Al-Qaeda. In Asia, Pakistan remained the major centre facilitating transit of terrorist cadres in and out of Afghanistan, as well as main disseminator of jihad cult through its madrasas which provided Islamic education to Muslims from all over the world. The radicalization and Islamicization of education in Pakistan had been continuing since the military regime of Zia-ul-Haq, when the Muslim seminaries received exclusive state patronage and thereby flourished in pursuit of what Zia-ul-Haq said was "a mission given by God to bring Islamic Order to Pakistan". These mosque-based schools became the breeding grounds for such militant religious organizations as Sipah-e-Sahaba Pakistan (SSP), pursuing strands of violent sectarian faith in Pakistan. Many such organizations were also requisitioned to participate in operations in Afghanistan. This in turn helped these religious militant groups to enlarge their political space within the Pakistani society as well as in its intelligence and security apparatus.

Once the Soviets withdrew from Afghanistan, the jihad as well as the mujahedins spilled over to the Kashmir valley and much of the MAK resources were diverted to regional conflicts worldwide, including Kashmir. The mujahideens thus found a new operational arena and a new mission to keep them engaged. Many Pakistani and Kashmiri groups used the training and operational infrastructure in Afghanistan and erstwhile Afghan veterans to undermine Indian control of Kashmir. The induction of Afghan veterans into the Kashmir conflict marked one of the bloodiest phases in Kashmiri militancy, beginning in the early 1990s. Most of these groups continued to grow with Al-Qaeda. Many terrorist groups operating from Pakistan became members of the International Islamic Front (IIF) spearheaded by Al-Qaeda under the 1998 Fatwa of the World Islamic Front for the Jihad Against the Jews and the Crusaders. This combination contributed to the reach and lethality of the groups, and changed the nature of militancy in South Asia significantly. The Kashmir issue got mixed up with the pan-Islamist extremist agenda and with most of the terrorist outfits, in addition to pursuing the separatist/irredentist objectives, increasingly also working at the behest of Osama bin Laden.

In the aftermath of September 11, 2001, Pakistan made a complete u-turn and became what Washington called "a frontline state" and a key ally in the global campaign against terror. It was ironic, especially as it was Pakistan which sponsored the Taliban in Afghanistan. The Taliban in Afghanistan owed much both to the terrorist groups operating in Pakistan as well as to the official establishment in Islamabad for its conception, empowerment and successes in many of its campaigns against what became the Northern Alliance, with whom it fought for control of most of Afghanistan. There was considerable evidence to suggest that the Taliban was being strongly supported by the Pakistani government led by Benazir Bhutto. Many of the top leaders in the Taliban were alumni of the Darul Uloom Islamia Binori Town Mosque in Karachi. It was in this mosque that many leaders from Taliban, Al-Qaeda, and groups from Pakistan and members of its intelligence agency, met and furthered their acquaintances. The head of the Binori Mosque Mufti Nizamuddin Shamzai was the spiritual mentor of Mullah Omar. As the Taliban was consolidating its position in Afghanistan, Al-Qaeda and Osama kept consolidating their hold on the Taliban, exploiting their reciprocal relationships. (When an US attack on the Taliban after September 11, 2001 became evident, Musharraf sent a team of Mullas led by Shamzai to Kandahar to persuade Mulla Omar to hand bin Laden over to the FBI.)

Given the complexity of the relationships among groups and individuals in the Afghanistan-Pakistan-Kashmir axis, it was not surprising to find that the immediate success of the "war on terror" did not alter the terrorist threat in the subcontinent. Thus terrorists continued to be active in most parts of the region especially in the Kashmir valley, which also remains as contentious an issue as ever between India and Pakistan in their bilateral relations. This has cast a shadow on the prospects of any long-term peace in the subcontinent. The militant infiltration into Kashmir from Pakistan across the Line of Control continued, threatening to become a flashpoint for a wider India-Pakistan conflict. Militancy in Kashmir has kept both India and Pakistan on the edge, especially as the threshold for major conflict—one involving terrorism—has been dangerously low in the region given the historic animosity between the nations. New Delhi, which fell victim to the Al-Qaeda brand of terrorism immediately after September 11, with attacks against the national Parliament in December 2001, also supported the global campaign against terror, and has been emphasizing the need to take into account the entire range and complexity of its international linkages, especially on the role of Pakistan's Inter Services Intelligence in pushing the insurgents inside the Indian territory. The December incident brought nuclear-armed neighbours to the brink of a major armed conflagration as both sides mobilized troops along the international border.

Pakistan has arrested several key Al-Qaeda operatives–Ramzi Binalshibh, Abu Zubaida and Khalid Sheikh Mohammed among them. But the nation continues to be a haven for global terrorism. Groups which had thus far confined their activities either to the separatist campaigns in Kashmir or to sectarian killings, have now come to take up the world jihad mantle at the behest of Al-Qaeda. Prominent among them are groups like Jaish-e-Mohammad (JeM), Sippah-e-Sahaba Pakistan (SSP), Lashkar-e-Jhangvi (LeJ), Laskar-e-Toiba (LeT) and Harkal-ul-Mujahidin (HuM). There are new formulations and configurations—the emerging link between the Hizbe Islami (HI) of Gulbuddin Heckmatyar and Jamaat-e-Islami (Jel) and Hizb-ul-Mujahid (HM) that is now consolidating a wave of resistance against the Hamid Karzai government in Afghanistan.

Many new groups with strategic links among existing ones have emerged, such as Lashkar-e-Omar (2002), the Muslim United Army (MUA): (2002); and 313 (2003). A wave of terrorist attacks tied to Al-Qaeda and its affiliates commenced after the formation of the new configuration, beginning with the killing of US journalist Daniel Pearl and the March 17, 2002 grenade attack on a church in Islamabad, in which five persons, including the wife of an American diplomat and her daughter were killed. The High Commissioner of Sri Lanka to Pakistan was injured among others. The May 8, 2002 killing of 11 French nationals, followed by the June attacks on the American Consulate in Karachi, as well as attacks on foreign tourists on the Karakoram Highway, are all believed to have been committed at the behest of the new configurations.

But sponsoring terrorism is like riding a tiger. Pakistan itself has to pay a heavy price for its support for the Taliban. Even though Musharraf demonstrated wisdom by supporting the US-led war on terror against the Taliban in neighbouring Afghanistan, the country continues to reel under a very complex web of terrorist activity, with greater radicalization of extremist groups. Karachi has reportedly emerged as a hub of Al-Qaeda activities after the collapse of the Taliban in Afghanistan, and has provided a safe haven and support, including financial support, to many Al-Qaeda fugitives.

Many Al-Qaeda operatives are also believed to have taken refuge in the tribal areas in western Pakistan and in the North West Frontier Province (NWFP) and the Federally Administered Tribal Areas

(FATA). Populated by conservative ethnic Pashtuns who share intimate religious and tribal linkages with their counterparts in Afghanistan, these tribes also hold vehement anti-Western and anti-American sentiments. The influx, at the least, has dangerously increased the terrorist threat to Pakistan. Reports that many others such as Jose Padilla, the one plotting a "dirty bomb" attack in Washington, transited through Pakistan even after September 11 had put the nation under intense international scrutiny.

Terrorism does bite the hand that feeds it.

8

South Asia: The Many Faces of Terror

Too often too many terrorism experts describe the "threat" as a transnational network with strong Islamic roots. There is some truth to this assertion. But South Asia, which in many ways is the original hub of post-modern terrorism, provides some of the most powerful arguments against viewing terrorism in such simple overarching terms. South Asian terrorism predates September 11. Moreover, its origins and dimensions are too localized to be explained purely in terms of a global terrorist brotherhood spreading its tentacles from Chechnya to the Molukus. The profile of terror in South Asia shows why attempts to implicate Islam for terrorism can be exaggerated. Here, terrorism is as much about a clash within a civilization as between civilizations.

While Kashmir continues to be the hub of terrorist activity, Islamic militancy in India is linked not only to the issue of liberation of Kashmir, but also to the rise in Hindu fundamentalism, which in recent years has kept the minority Muslims in a state of insecurity. Several incidents demonstrate this assumption, such as the riots in Gujurat and the latest series of bombings in Mumbai, the commercial capital of India, to name a few.

The emerging profile of some of the terrorists arrested, for example, in connection with the attack on the Indian Parliament and the recent blasts in Mumbai suggest the fallacy of linking terrorism in South Asia exclusively with external sources. Even as most of the previous terrorist acts were blamed on Pakistan or its militant proxies, the emerging pattern now points to indigenous Islamic radicals, many of them educated, middle-class professionals. An example is Mohammed Abdul Mateen, an affable if somewhat bookish young doctor working in the forensics department of a Government medical college. This has sparked the fear that "rising Hindu nationalism may be prompting a small but radical fringe of Muslims to violence". For the series of bombings in Mumbai, of the 23 arrested, there were five engineers, three physicians, one business-school graduate, two college graduates with multiple degrees and a doctoral student who had just completed his dissertation. There is also evidence that these people had kept a keen interest on the September 11 attacks.

Most forms of terrorism in South Asia predate September 11 and have nothing to do with Islam. In Sri Lanka, the decades-old Tamil separatist campaign spearheaded by the LTTE claimed over 64,000 lives until it took a break, as the Tigers were persuaded to engage in Norwegian-brokered peace talks. India's Northeast—composed of the multi-ethnic and multicultural states of Assam, Arunachal Pradesh, Manipur, Meghalaya, Mizoram, Nagaland, Tripura and Sikkim—has been the theatre of a variety of militant campaigns. These are mostly old-fashioned ethno-political secessionist movements, which thrive by straddling international boundaries between India, Bhutan, China, Burma, Bangladesh and Nepal. Comprising a number of unique ethnic communities living in close proximity, these states, except Sikkim, have witnessed considerable and at times the worst forms of ethnic cleansing.

But in the Indian heartland, it is essentially left-wing extremist (Naxalite) groups which continue to wreck havoc. Their strongholds include Jharkhand, Bihar and Andhra Pradesh Orissa, Chhattisgarh, Madhya Pradesh, Maharashtra, West Bengal and Uttar Pradesh. There has been evidence of coordination among different Naxal groups within India and outside, especially with the Maoist insurgents in Nepal. The objective is to create what the groups call a "compact revolutionary zone" from Nepal to the Southern Indian state of Andhra Pradesh. In 2001, Naxal organizations of four South Asian countries—India, Nepal, Bangladesh and Sri Lanka—joined hands to form an umbrella organization named the Coordination Committee of Maoist Parties and Organisations of South Asia (CCOMPOSA). Their goal is to "unify and coordinate the activities of the Maoist parties and organizations in South Asia".

Most of these groups do not have any specific agenda, rather these groups engaged in violence to protest against what they perceive as prevailing injustice and inequality in the system. The groups have successfully infiltrated and embedded themselves in the tribal/jungle environment where illiteracy is rampant along with a lack of basic facilities and virtual absence of any civic governance.

The Maoist insurgency in Nepal has reached unprecedented levels with coordinated countrywide terrorist strikes. In the following months, the Maoists appeared to have consolidated their position by declaring the formation of a "Central People's Government" running parallel administrations in their strongholds, such as in Rolpa, Rukum, Jajarkot and Salyan districts. The Maoists have been demanding the abolition of monarchy and turning Nepal into a Republic. After large-scale violence in the year 2002, peace initiatives led to the Government and the Maoists declaring a ceasefire on January 29, 2003. But this was jettisoned unilaterally by the insurgents in August 2003, triggering another spate of violence. The Government has now declared the Communist Party of Nepal (Maoists) a terrorist organization.

Terrorism in South Asia has strong local roots. To be sure, armed violence in the northeast of India has long had significant connections with insurgents and small arms traffickers outside. Part of the insurgency and militancy in this area can be linked to refugees from Bangladesh, who threatened to disturb the local demography. New Delhi has also accused Pakistan's Inter Services Intelligence Agency and the erstwhile Taliban regime of involvement in terrorist-criminal networks in the northeast. This has been linked to a rise in the instances of Islamic terrorism in the northeast by such groups as the Muslim United Liberation Tigers of Assam (MULTA), Muslim United Liberation Front of Assam (MULFA), People's Liberation Front (PLF), International Liberation Army (ILA), Muslim Security Force (MSF), Liberation of Islamic Tiger Force (LITF), Muslim Security Council of Assam (MSCA), United Liberation Militia of Assam (ULMA). some of these groups have established connections with Kashmiri Islamic terrorist organizations.

In some cases, local terrorist networks do thrive with foreign support. Most of the terrorist groups active in Kashmir, namely the Hizb-ul-Mujahideen (HuM), are linked to the Jamaat-e-Islami (JeI) in Pakistan; the Lashkar-e-Toiba (LeT), the armed wing of the Markaz-ud-Da'awa-wal-Irshad (MuDI); the Harkat-ul-Jihad-e-Islami (HuJI) and the Harkat-ul-Mujahideen (HuM, formerly the Harkat-ul-Ansar), are linked to the Jamaat-e-Ulema, Pakistan, while the Al Badr; and the Jaish-e-Mohammed (JeM) groups are based in Pakistan. Similarly, terrorism in Bangladesh came to international attention in 2001, with a reported influx of Taliban and Al-Qaeda cadres from Afghanistan. The leader of a local terrorist group, Fazlul Rahman of Harkat-ul-Jihad-al-Islami (HuJI), was one of the signatories to bin

Laden's February 23, 1998 Fatwa on "world jihad". There have been reports of young Muslim radicals from Malaysia and Indonesia and ones belonging to Jemaah Islamiah taking refuge in Cox's Bazar and Chittagong and maintaining contacts with local Muslim groups.

But Pakistan also offers a good reason for viewing South Asian terrorism as a local phenomenon and as the by-product of a clash within a civilization. Terrorist violence in Pakistan is sectarian in nature. The Sunni groups include the Sipah-e-Sahaba Pakistan (SSP) and Lashkar-e-Jhangvi (LeJ); and a militant Wahabi tribal group, the Tehreek-e-Nafaz-e-Shariat-e-Mohammadi (TNSM). The Shia groups are the Tehreek-e-Jaferia Pakistan (TJP) and Sipah-e-Mohammed Pakistan (SMP). Recent incidents of sectarian violence have involved a wave of attacks against the Shi'as and most significantly the killing of SSP leader Azam Tariq. Some analysts believe that, by redirecting Pakistan's internal security resources, this increase in sectarian violence may ease pressure on Al-Qaeda and so allow that group to operate more freely.

9

Palestinians as "Terrorists"

Soon after the September 11 attacks, Robert Fisk, a long-time observer of the Middle East, wrote a column about "The wickedness and awesome cruelty of a crushed and humiliated people". He contended that "this is not the war of democracy versus terror that the world will be asked to believe in the coming days. It is also about American missiles smashing into Palestinian homes and US helicopters firing missiles into a Lebanese ambulance in 1996 and American shells crashing into a village called Qana and about a Lebanese militia—paid and uniformed by America's Israeli ally—hacking and raping and murdering their way through refugee camps".

A little over a year after the September 11 attacks, Saudi Crown Prince Abdullah Bin Abdel Aziz telephoned President George W. Bush. The Saudi leader was reported to have reminded the US President: "The Palestinian issue, which concerns all Arabs and Muslims, is a source of instability in the region". In a message to the OIC meeting in Kuala Lumpur in October 2003, Kofi Annan, the Secretary-General of the UN, said the Palestinian people were suffering under "a harsh and prolonged occupation" and no one should be surprised at their feelings of humiliation, anger and despair. "However, suicide bombings, in which hundreds of Israeli civilians have been indiscriminately killed, are not acceptable". "These acts of terrorism, abhorred and rejected by all of you, defile and damage even the most legitimate cause".

Malaysia's Mahathir Mohamad was less subtle in linking the Palestinian issue with the scourge of international terrorism. "It is reasonable to believe if there is no Palestinian issue, if the Palestinians are not being oppressed and children killed, the anger of the Arabs and Muslims would not be there or would be much less. "Certainly there would not be those who would be willing to kill themselves in the horrible manner as in the attack of September 11", he added.

There thus is a widespread view that the lack of justice for the Palestinians is a root cause of terrorism. In fact, all parties in the war on terrorism acknowledge the link. But they do so for different reasons.

Count among them Osama bin-laden. An Al-Qaeda website, claims to be dedicated to the "full liberation of the Palestine land". Soon after the terrorist attack in Mombasa, an Al-Qaeda statement claiming responsibility asserted that the liberation of Palestine is a "central issue" in the attack.

Both Yasser Arafat and Ariel Sharon agree with Osama that there is a link between the Palestinians and terror. But for Sharon, the "Palestinian issue" that feeds terrorism is not the lack of Palestinian statehood, but the terrorist acts of Hamas suicide bombers. Since September 11, Israel has joined the rank of many nations that have sought to portray liberation struggles as terrorist movements. The neo-con group, Project for the American Century, in an open letter to Bush on April 3, 2002, gave a full airing to the Israeli government perspective. Reminding the President that "Israel is fighting the same war ... [as the US] on international terrorism," it described Arafat and the leadership of the Palestinian Authority as "one spoke of the terrorist network". The letter denounced the "mistaken view" held by critics in the United States, Europe and the Arab world that the US and the Bush administration bore "some responsibility for the lack of political progress between Israel and the Palestinians". It even cited Colin Powell to the effect that the present crisis in the Middle East was not due to "the absence of a political way forward" on the Palestinian-Israeli conflict, but to "terrorism ..., terrorism in its rawest form". Finally, it urged the US not to go for negotiations which might be seen as a product of "product of terrorism or conducted under the threat of terrorist attack", for that would send the wrong signal that the US does not have "the necessary courage to fight terrorism in all its forms".

The Bush administration seems to side with this Israeli view at least in one important respect. "There will never be peace so long as there is terror, and all of us should fight terror. I'd like to see Chairman Arafat denounce the terror".

In fact, Arafat has done exactly that. Responding to such attempts to link the Palestinian issue with terrorism in the Israeli way, Arafat launched into a sharp attack on Osama. In December 2002, he accused the Al-Qaeda leader of "exploiting" the Palestinian issue to justify his terrorist activities. Claiming to be the "first Arab leader to stand up to bin Laden'", Arafat told the *Sunday Times* of London: "I'm telling him directly not to hide behind the Palestinian cause". As Arafat put it: "Why is bin Laden talking about Palestine now? He never helped us. He was working in another, completely different area and against our interests". Arafat rejected all accusation of his movement's links with any international terrorist network. Israel, he insisted, knew fully that there were "no relations between the Al-Qaeda and Palestine" but was using the issue to justify attacks on Palestinians.

Yet, for Bush, while the war on terror creates opportunities for resolving the Palestinian issue, it must be waged first before the latter can be attempted. This is different from the view that maintains that the resolution of the Palestinian issue brings America nearer to victory in its war on terror. Bush also insists that terror, including Palestinian terror, must be defeated first. "He has insisted pretty consistently that the Palestinians must act first. They must stop acts of terrorism, he has often said. They must move toward democratic government and the rule of law, he said June 24, before he would call on the Israelis to do things in return. Who must act first is critical. Insisting that both parties act simultaneously means, in effect, more pressure on Israel than on the Palestinians. Insisting that the Palestinians move first means much more pressure on the Palestinians than Israel."

For the rest of the world, the link between the Palestinian issue and international terrorism is less complicated.

In an open letter to Bush dated September 15, 2001, Chandra Muzaffar, a noted Malaysian politician and civil society leader advocate, noted:

> The policies of the US government in the Middle East in the last 50 odd years, and especially in the last decade, have created so much frustration and desperation among the Arab masses that it has set the stage for terrorism. Palestine more than any other conflict epitomises this sense of hopelessness and helplessness. Because of the United States' intimate relationship with Israel, Palestinians and Arabs are convinced that they cannot expect even a modicum of justice from your government. The brutal suppression of the second Intifada in the last few months which witnessed Israel unleash the full fury of state terror upon a humiliated and subjugated people was perhaps 'the last straw that broke the camel's back'. In the eyes of the victims of Israeli aggression and occupation, their oppressor could not have

> embarked upon such merciless suppression without the support and solidarity of the US.

This is neither an outlandish suggestion nor is it exceptional. Lee Kuan Yew, not an enemy of Israel, also finds a link between terrorism and the Palestinian issue. In his keynote speech to the 1st International Institute for Strategic Studies Asia Security Conference on May 31, 2002, he argued: "The majority of Muslims who are moderates are caught in between (1) their sympathy for and identification with the Palestinians and anger against the Israelis, and (2) their desire for a peaceful life of growth and progress. To resolve the problem of terrorism, the US and others must support the tolerant non-militant Muslims so that they will prevail". This would presumably mean a one-sided American policy.

Against this backdrop, what sort of policy has the Bush administration pursued as the Middle East peacemaker? A few days before the war against Bin Laden broke out, President Bush announced that "the idea of a Palestinian state has always been part of the US vision in the Middle East, as long as the right of Israel to exist is respected". Now, nearly three months after Mr. Bush's Rose Garden speech in which he offered a vision of "two states living side by side in peace"—and spoke openly of "Palestine".

Soon thereafter, on April 30, Bush formally presented the "roadmap for peace" to Israel and the Palestinians. The Palestinians were asked to rein in militant activity. Israel was to end attacks on the civilian areas and the demolition of Palestinian homes and property, and dismantle settlement outposts erected since the establishment of the present Israeli government. Later, in the second stage of the first phase the Israelis were supposed to stop all settlement activities. This was to be followed by the second phase of the roadmap (from June 2003 to December 2003) during which emphasis would be on Palestinian political reform and security cooperation. During this phase, Israel was to withdraw from the areas it occupied after September 2000 and freeze all settlement activities.

The newly-appointed Prime Minister of Palestine Mahmood Abbas was able to secure a three-month ceasefire from the Hamas. During the first 51 days of ceasefire the militant Palestinian groups undertook no violent acts. But the suicide attacks did not stop.

Neither the Israelis nor the Palestinian moderates could manage to rein in the extremists, which would have required an Israeli government to compel the militant settlers on the West Bank to leave. As long as Yasser Arafat remained in charge of the Palestinian Authority (PA), Israel was convinced that the PA would not be able to deliver on the security requirements of the roadmap. Not much effort was made to restrain the Israelis in their retaliation with Palestinian territory and stop the settlement activity. In the end, both sides failed to keep their ends of the bargain. Israel continued to demolish Palestinians homes, destroy Palestinian farms and confiscate Palestinian land for the purpose of building more Jewish settlements on the land it had occupied in 1967. Although it did, on a few occasions, dismantle a few "illegal outposts", it did not freeze construction of all settlements. Instead, it built more Jewish settlements. Moreover, it pushed ahead on a "security wall" during the ceasefire, a wall which would leave Palestinians trapped in small ghettos—reminiscent of the South African Bantustans—but allow Jewish settlers complete freedom in the occupied territories. The Israeli hint of killing or expelling Yasser Arafat from Palestine marked the final nail in the coffin of the road map.

Why then did the road map die? Because from the very outset, it was based on the same self-serving and false logic that the war on terror must be won before the Palestinians can have their own state. The war on terror did not facilitate the settlement of the Palestinian issue. The terrorist labelling instead might have killed the roadmap. Although the Bush administration refused to label Arafat as a terrorist, it continued to agree with Israel that the war on terror must be won first and to this end, the Palestinian Authority must denounced terror. On June 4, 2003, Bush argued that the downfall of Saddam would pave the way for peace in the Middle East. The war, he argued, had led to a new recognition that the defeat of Saddam was a defeat for terrorism and this would "make it easier for a Palestinian state to emerge".

Yet, the war on terror, which includes an attack on Iraq, and Israel's massive retaliation strategy in the occupied territories, and which implicates Palestinians as terrorists rather than interlocutors, did not remove the Palestinian issue as a source of terror. The US must seek to address the Palestinian issue first as a way of dampening the source of terror and achieving victory in the war, after having won the military engagement in Afghanistan and Iraq.

Sources

Robert Fisk, "The wickedness and awesome cruelty of a crushed and humiliated people", September 12, 2001, http://news.independent.co.uk/world/americas/story.jsp?story=93623

http://www.newamericancentury.org/Bushletter-040302.htm

http://www.metimes.com/2K1/issue2001-39/reg/palestinian_issue_a.htm

http://www.channelnewsasia.com/stories/afp_asiapacific/view/52543/1/.html

http://www.palestinecampaign.org/archives.asp?xid=417

http://www.foxnews.com/story/0,2933,49324,00.html

http://www.hinduonnet.com/thehindu/2002/12/16/stories/2002121602691400.htm

http://www.usnews.com/usnews/opinion/baroneweb/mb_020628.htm

Zachary Abuza, *Militant Islam in Southeast Asia: Crucible of Terror* (Boulder, CO: Lynne Rienner, 2003)

http://sg.news.yahoo.com/020530/57/2qiur.html

http://weekly.ahram.org.eg/2001/555/op3.htm

http://www.csmonitor.com/2002/0617/p01s03-uspo.html

http://www.usembassy.it/file2003_06/alia/A3060404.htm

John Mintz, 'al Qaeda website calls Israel new target, in 'newsbytes', December 6, 2002; Chandra Muzzaffar, 'Bush's War Against Terrorism: Be Cautious!', http://www.weeklyholiday.net/120702/edit.html

Jimmy Carter, 'This Will Not Be A Just War', *Guardian*, March 12, 2003.

America's Fears and the Fear of America

What is this monster that has just grasped you, completely changing your personality? Altering your being?!

Rodney W. 8th Grade

www.kidsforpeace.org, http://www.peaceinc.org/pledge/definitions/fear.htm

"America's unprecedented power scares the world, and the Bush administration has only made it worse."

Fareed Zakaria, *Newsweek*, March 24, 2003

"Can a world power provide global leadership on the basis of fear and anxiety"?

Zbigniew Brzezinski, *Washington Post*, November 15–16, 2003

10

Unipolar World, Unilateral Hegemon

Academic specialists of international affairs have long debated how global power structures shape peace and stability. A leader among them, American political scientist Kenneth Waltz, believed that a world with only two superpowers is more stable that a world with many. Hence, the Cold War was more orderly than, say 19th century Europe, when several great powers vied for influence and unleashed many destructive wars. A multipolar world, he argued, is messy, alliances are hard to predict and difficult to maintain. It is difficult to know who is doing what to whom.

When the Cold War ended, another American political scientist, John Mearsheimer, resurrected Waltz's thesis. He argued that with the return of the world to a multipolar structure, we should be going "back to the future". In short, Europe's future might well resemble its past. Aaron Friedberg, a fellow political scientist at Princeton, echoed this view in analysing prospects for Asia. Although some scholars challenged the Mearsheimer thesis, most accepted that too many great powers will make the world a more dangerous place than two.

What no one foresaw then, was that we were heading for a world with only one superpower, not many. America's leadership in swiftly expelling Saddam's forces from Kuwait ushered in what columnist Charles Krauthammer called a "unipolar moment". But even he himself could scarcely predict that moment would turn out to be an "era".

Does American primacy make the world more stable? Yes, if you believe the neo-cons. For them, American hegemony is of a special kind; even with a dose of unilateralism, it's the best guarantee of world order. This is because America cherishes and propagates values—democracy and free market among them, which are good for the entire mankind. A unipolar world, why even an American imperium, is not only moral, it is also the best guarantee of stability that we are likely to have.

Events since September 11 may provide some ammunition to those who believe that a unipolar world order is conducive to international peace and stability. For example, renewed American strategic engagement in Southeast Asia to counter terrorism would be viewed by many regional governments, if not their peoples generally, as a positive force for regional stability. American hegemony has been strengthened so much that it now acts as a significant check on regional conflicts. For example, by consolidating its influence over both India and Pakistan, America has acquired an unprecedented ability to restrain their rivalry, one of the most dangerous flashpoints in Asia and the world.

In the past, hegemony did not prevent the US from acting multilaterally. It was a victorious United States after World War II which presided over a prolific era of multilateral institution-building (including the UN and the Bretton Woods institutions). This became the basis of the theory of "hegemonic stability", pioneered by Robert Gilpin, Charles Kindleberger, and Stephen Krasner among others. This theory conceptualized how America promoted global order by offering public good in vital areas (such as free trade and security). But the positive linkage between hegemony and multilateral cooperation has been challenged in the post-September 11 world. This is evident from the US attitude towards coalition-building during the Afghanistan war. George W. Bush did not replicate the "New World Order" approach that his father had employed against Saddam Hussein in 1990. Instead of collective security, the US invoked the right of national self-defence under the UN charter to bypass direct Security Council authorization for the conduct of the military campaign. Learning from Kosovo where alliance warfare had proven cumbersome, the US also shunned NATO's direct involvement, although the alliance had invoked its collective defence provision for the first time in history in support of the US.

While the international community was generally supportive of the US position in attacking the Taliban, each of America's key regional allies have demanded and secured something in return for their backing for the US. (This was in contrast to the situation during the Gulf War of 1991, when the US got its allies, Japan and Germany in particular, to pay for most of the war costs.) China and Russia were quick to press for an American understanding that domestic insurgencies should be viewed as a terrorist, rather than human rights, issue. India secured American backing for its own war against terrorism involving Pakistani-supported Kashmir militants.

Hopes that September 11 may create a new basis for multilateralism proved short-lived. The war produced a nominal improvement in great power relations. But here too seeds of discord were already evident. The warmth in US-Russian relations sparked by Putin's sympathy and support for the US did not prevent a mad dash to Afghanistan by Russian troops soon after its liberation from the Taliban. The terrorist attacks diverted attention from Sino-US tensions, eased by China's support, albeit qualified, for the US anti-terrorist campaign. But China's sense of military vulnerability in the Taiwan Straits could only be aggravated by the awesome display of US power projection in Afghanistan. Beijing could not have been happy with the haste with which the Japanese government pushed through legislation to enable its navy (in a supporting role) to enter the waters of the Indian Ocean for the first time since World War II in war time. In Europe, while British and West European support for the US was predictably forthcoming after September 11, the Blair government probably surprised itself with its exceptionally strong backing of the Bush Administration. And the initial US-European consensus shows many signs of stress, with growing disagreements over the Palestinian question as well as the planned American attack on Iraq, itself an extension of America's war on terror.

The dangers of American unilateralism have been highlighted in a new book by Joseph Nye, *The Paradox of American Power: Why the World's Only Superpower Can't Go it Alone*. Going against common practice, Nye dismisses the characterisation of the current world power structure in terms of the categories "multipolar" or "unipolar". Multipolarity is the wrong term because it assumes rough parity among several powers. Unipolarity is also wrong because it assumes US' ability to get what it wants in all areas of world politics. Instead, Nye employs the metaphor of a "complex three dimensional chess game". In this model, the first or the top dimension is military power, which can be accurately described as a unipolar configuration. The second dimension is economic, which is more multipolar, with the US, Japan, and Europe and in the future, China, being the key actors.

It is the third layer which is the greatest challenge. It consists of transnational relations, or the realm of the borderless world, which to a significant extent lies outside of government control. In this realm operate the powerful and sometimes dark forces of international relations: global financiers who can transfer billions at the stroke of a key, terrorists who brought down the World Trade Center like a house of cards, and hackers who disrupt websites of the most powerful corporations and governments. "On this bottom board", argues Professor Nye, power is widely dispersed, and it makes no sense to speak of uni-polarity, multipolarity or hegemony".

This leads Nye to make his major point. Because of the complexity of the challenges it faces and the changing nature of transnational relations, the US cannot go it alone in international affairs. In dealing with a whole range of vital issues that challenge international security, ranging from international financial stability, global climate change, transnational, post-modern terrorism, infectious diseases and drug trafficking, "America must mobilize international coalitions to address shared threats and challenges". Nye concludes that the US is likely to remain the leading power in world politics well into the 21st century, but this is contingent on a number of factors: the US will not suffer from economic or social decay, the US will not turn unilateralist or isolationist, that it will maintain its military strength without being over-militarised, and that the US will define its national interest "in a broad and far-sighted way that incorporates global interests".

Nye's arguments against US unilateralism, persuasive as they might be, are largely utilitarian and American-centric. What it says is multilateralism, the US could lose its influence and fail to realise its interests and achieve its goals. This ignores the moral and subjective case against US unilateralism from the perspective of the rest of the international community. American unilateralism is not just bad for America, but for the whole world. Unilateral power is power without legitimacy. And power without legitimacy not only damages the hegemon's interests, but also the collective interests of the whole world.

11

1991 and 2001

When America fired the first salvo in its war against terrorism by attacking targets in Afghanistan in October, 2001, the parallels and differences with the last major US offensive in the Middle East could not be more striking. Then, as now, the US was the world's sole superpower with a huge military advantage over its enemy. America led in the battlefield as well as in the diplomatic arena. Then, as now, the US embraced multilateralism to legitimize the offensive and ensure its success by securing material and financial support from other nations.

But the differences overshadow the similarities. The 1990 Gulf War was fought against a clearly identifiable enemy and on terrain highly favourable to large-scale conventional operations. The impending war in Afghanistan will be fought as much against the terrain as against the terrorist.

Even more serious differences mark the diplomatic and political context. Bush Sr.'s New World Order was provoked by an act of aggression against one small nation, albeit a moderate oil-rich one, by its large neighbour. The war against Afghanistan is prompted by an attack on America itself. This fact, and the horrific scenes viewed around the world of large airliners smashing into the Twin Towers in New York should make it easier for America to secure international backing for its War Against Terror. Ironically, however, President George W. Bush could find it surprisingly more difficult to replicate the New World Order coalition brilliantly crafted by his father.

The terrorist attacks on the US prompted the US to rediscover multilateralism, but other nations will not easily forget the administration's aggressive unilateralism in the first months in office. Bush Sr. himself is reported to have admonished his son's administration for its past go-it-alone policy while welcoming the current shift. Against this backdrop, Bush's embrace of multilateralism seems self-serving and utilitarian.

Despite the about-face, there remain major differences between George W. Bush's multilateral approach and his father's New World

Order coalition. The latter's campaign against Iraq was bankrolled by allies such as Japan and Germany, while his son's campaign can be best described as "pork-barrel multilateralism". In exchange for political and logistics support, Bush Jr. has had to dish out significant goodies to allied governments. Pakistan, critical to Bush's retaliation against Afghanistan, gets its nuclear sanctions lifted in return for its support for the US. President Megawati of Indonesia, the leader of the world's largest Islamic nation, hence of considerable symbolic value to the administration, has returned from Washington with promises of substantial new economic and military aid.

Even as world leaders made a beeline to the White House to offer sympathy and support, they also carry misgivings in their heart and messages of caution in their mouth. And most want something in return for their support for the US military offensive. America's European allies are wary of Bush's overly belligerent tone. While core allies such as UK and Canada have offered troops, and NATO has for the first time in its history invoked its collective security clause, France has expressed reservations and urged a more political and diplomatic approach to transnational terrorism. Many nations, both in the West and in the Middle East want the US to temper its backing for Israel. And they hope that the US will from now on be less disposed to strategic unilateralism.

America cannot win the War Against Terror by military means alone. In changing its military doctrine and strategy to cope with transnational terrorism, the US must change its foreign policy approach in fundamental ways.

Southeast Asia provides an important example of the limitations of a purely strategic approach. Here, the US counter-terrorism programme has been overwhelmingly strategic; military assistance, economic aid and security agreements have not been backed by efforts to address what is perceived in Southeast Asia as fundamental root causes of contemporary Islamic radicalism: poverty, inequality, and the issue of Palestine. While the post-September 11 milieu has seen a dramatic increase in American hard power, there has been a noticeable erosion of American soft power. Many US actions on the world stage—Iraq, withdrawal from the Kyoto Protocol, the international war crimes tribunal and so on—have led to a perception that US foreign policy lacks "legitimacy".

Southeast Asian countries are less worried about the US retreating from the region, but about its assertive primacy and unilateralism. Support for the US-led war on terror is a double-edged sword. While it allows countries to gain access to US resources; military and economic, and helps them to conduct their own war on terror, it is also risky and costly in the domestic front, where the US role is viewed with considerable misgivings. Southeast Asian governments have to maintain a delicate balance in supporting the US while maintaining domestic cohesion. In a multi-ethnic milieu, Southeast Asian governments risk domestic and friction and backlash unless they maintain a careful distance from the excesses of US unilateralism and its pro-Israeli stance.

12

Dubya's Dangerous, Divisive Doctrine

The new American strategic doctrine of "pre-emptive" strikes enunciated one year after September 11 provokes more discord internationally than it catalyses accord domestically. Past presidential doctrines have helped American leaders to mobilize domestic support and organize broad international coalitions. The Bush Doctrine has become more divisive than any previous post-war pronouncement.

Past presidential doctrines have signalled major shifts in US strategic policy, underscored new dangers and outlined new strategies for coping with them. The Truman Doctrine presaged the containment of the Soviet Union. The Nixon Doctrine announced the US disengagement from mainland Asia. The Carter Doctrine signalled US determination to secure Persian Gulf oil by any means necessary including military force. And the Reagan Doctrine promised the rollback of Soviet geopolitical advance in the Third World.

The new Bush Doctrine has a simple premise: the US will use force, pre-emptively if necessary, to deal with regimes which pose a threat to US strategic interests, especially by sponsoring terrorism or acquiring weapons of mass destruction.

In reality, however, like the war against terror, the Bush Doctrine is expansive (as well as expensive) and all-encompassing. It is defined by issue-linkages: getting rid of weapons of mass destruction requires "regime change"; regime change in turn cannot be accomplished without military occupation of the target state. The doctrine has no clear boundary markers or exit strategies. Its limits are set not by international norms or allies' reactions but by its author's questionable capacity for self-restraint.

Iraq is a good case where grand presidential doctrines can be unhelpful and dangerous. While doctrines help focus attention and mobilize resources against a particular threat, they also limit flexibility. The Iraqi case is in many respects exceptional. Had the American president chosen to focus on Iraq as a one-off thing, without presenting it as part of a sweeping geopolitical framework, the international community might have less reason to oppose it.

The main objection to the Bush Doctrine is the prospect of Washington securing for itself a blank cheque to strike any regime which falls foul of it by acquiring weapons of mass destruction or through some other pretext. Assurances of maintaining a high threshold and promises not to act casually or irresponsibly, are not enough, given the Bush Administration's tendency towards unilateralism.

The real reason for discomfort about the Bush Doctrine is not pre-emption *per se*. Many states would be willing to accept the pre-emptive use of force against a rogue regime (Saddam Hussein more than qualifies) if it was pursued through legitimate means, which in the present international context, can only mean authorization by the UN Security Council.

The Bush Doctrine would have caused less of a stir had a pre-emptive strategy been outlined earlier or without other steps taken by the Administration which show a clear disregard for multilateralism. For instance, no one complained when in the 1980s the US developed a pre-emptive strategy to seize Middle Eastern air bases (and oil fields) against an impending Soviet attack (a hypothetical scenario). Things are different today. The list of US disregard for multilateral agreements is long and growing: the International Criminal Court, the Kyoto Protocol, the ABM Treaty. The Bush Doctrine is part of a pattern of unilateralist behaviour of the current Administration which raises several concerns. What is the threshold of pre-emption? What sort of evidence would be needed to justify a military strike? What is the limit to such strikes? Will it be proportional? Will it involve political control of the target country? (The Administration's plan to rule Iraq with a military regime suggests yes.)

There is also the conflation of American strategic, humanitarian and economic goals. An occupation of Iraq, ostensibly to eliminate weapons of mass destruction and human rights abuses, will also put under American control one of the world's largest proven reserves of oil. The absence of a clear separation between international purposes and national interests sharpens the perception of the Bush Doctrine as a self-serving approach that could undermine international order.

The international community is worried that the Bush Doctrine would lead to hasty military action, without exhausting all possible diplomatic means. The developing world is worried about its flouting of the sovereignty principle. This is less of a concern in Europe, itself a champion of the doctrine of humanitarian intervention, which sanctions the use of force to protect the lives of people ruled by repressive regimes. But to European minds, eliminating the threat of weapons of mass destruction does not qualify as a "just cause" for military action in the same way as abuse of human rights does.

The irony of the Bush Doctrine is that no one disputes the worthiness of its goal, i.e., the removal of a heinous regime which poses as great a threat to the international community as it does to its own citizens. But in international politics the end does not always justify the means.

To be sure, the National Security Strategy document does mention the importance of alliances and the need for multilateral action. But no one takes this seriously, least of all US allies in Europe. Already it has produced the most serious rift in US-German relations since World War II. The German opposition to the planned US attack on Iraq might be prompted by domestic compulsions. But Germany is not alone in Europe in opposing US policy towards Iraq. Europeans generally complain about the Bush administration "instrumental" multilateralism, which they contrast with the "principled" multilateralism (based on rule of law and diplomacy) of European states and regional institutions.

Asian countries, whose approach to multilateralism may be more pragmatic than principled, have in the main chosen to keep quiet about their discomfort with the pre-emptive strategy so as not to complicate their ties with Washington. However Asia, like Europe, has much to lose from an assertive American unilateralism. While discreet silence at the implications of the Bush Doctrine might serve the short-term interests of Asian countries that need American backing against the terrorist threat, in the long term they might well find the consequences of US unilateralism to be negative. After all, any doctrine of unilateral intervention or pre-emptive strike is more likely to be tried in hot spots in Asia rather than in Europe.

13

Why a Second Gulf War Is Not in Asia's Interest

As the international community prepares for war in the Persian Gulf, the escalating crisis in the Korean peninsula further undercuts the legitimacy of a US military strike on Saddam and creates new dilemmas for Asian countries in offering support for the US.

A second Gulf War may still be avoided, though no one seems to be betting on this outcome. But Asia has little to gain from a US-Iraq confrontation.

First, many Asian countries, like the international community at large, are still not convinced of the rationale behind a US strike on Iraq. The Bush administration claims that war is necessary to rid the world of a regime that threatens US and global security by quietly but surely building up an arsenal of deadly weapons of mass destruction. Many Asians sense other motives. Explanations include this being a personal family vendetta, or a continuation of domestic election politics, now with an eye on the re-election campaign of George W. Bush. Still others see it as a ploy to secure firm US control over the vast oil resources of the Middle East.

Second, Asian countries are wary of the economic consequences of a second Gulf War. Much depends on the actual duration and course of the war. A short and swift campaign will cause minimum disruption to oil supply and raise world oil prices only temporarily. The Saudis have agreed to compensate for oil shortages caused by the war. The US will move quickly to resume Iraqi oil production after occupying the country, provided its oil wells have not been destroyed by Iraqi forces.

Chances of a quick American victory in Iraq are by no means far-fetched. The Iraqi army today is only a shadow of its 1990 form when it quickly overran Kuwait but was easily brushed aside by the US-led coalition. Iraq has no defences to test American airpower. US forces are now much more familiar with Iraqi terrain and combat conditions in the Gulf than they were in 1990. And as seen in Afghanistan,

American war technology has moved leaps and bounds in critical areas such as long range power projection, surveillance and targeting capabilities, information warfare, the use of special forces, and improved command and control systems.

Achieving a quick and decisive victory with minimum casualties in Iraq will be critical in deciding domestic US and international political opposition to the war. A prolonged campaign with large-scale civilian casualties will affect American morale, fuel domestic anti-war sentiment and aggravate anti-US feelings around the world. It would also further alienate US allies in Europe and Asia who are already quite sceptical of the purpose and merit of the Bush administration's obsession with Saddam.

Moreover, having the capacity to overwhelm Saddam's forces does not itself lend legitimacy to the war against Saddam in the eyes of Asian countries. It will be easier for them to support the US if Washington returns to the Security Council and seeks formal authorization for a strike on Iraq after the submission of the report of the UN inspectors. But it is unlikely that the UN arms inspectors in Iraq would come up with a smoking gun that would justify Security Council authorization of war. And it is not certain that Russia and China will support a UN mandate to oust Saddam militarily even if the US seeks it. An American strike without UN authorization adds to the declining comfort level of Asian with the current American strategic posture.

Moreover, Asian governments face the possibility of a popular Muslim backlash against US interests, which would also affect the stability of regional countries who are closely allied with the US. This may not amount to revolutionary upsurges in Asia, but in multi-ethnic societies of Southeast Asia, governments could face heightened internal opposition for their silence on, or support for, a US strike on Iraq.

An American strike on Iraq could also undermine the war on terror, which for Asian governments is a much more urgent and important challenge. Many Asian analysts already see the Iraqi issue as a huge distraction from the war on terrorism. There is no evidence linking the Saddam Hussein regime with Al-Qaeda. A military confrontation with Iraq would further divert attention and resources from US support for counter-terrorism and undermine the fledging international cooperation against terror.

The escalating crisis in the Korean peninsula is another reason why the US obsession with Saddam is bad for Asia. Iraq was the primary reason behind the axis of evil formulation, which aggravated North Korean insecurity. American belligerence towards the axis of evil and its disdain for multilateral action might have given North Korea a reason and an opportunity to raise the ante by withdrawing from the non-proliferation regime. Preoccupied with Iraq, the administration was not prepared for the dramatic turn in the Korean conflict.

North Korea's nuclear programme is more advanced than Iraq's. Pyongyang poses a more immediate threat to its neighbour than Iraq. Since the main reason for going to war against Saddam is its programme of weapons of mass destruction, should not the same logic apply to North Korea? Targeting Iraq while offering a hand of compromise to North Korea further undermines the legitimacy of the US military strike on Iraq.

The North Korean crisis is a timely reminder that Asia's old conflicts continue to pose a severe threat to regional stability and are not to be ignored in the current preoccupation with terrorism. It's in Asia's interest that US pursues an active policy to contain North Korea's nuclear ambitions; the consequence of failure would be catastrophic, including the possible nuclearization of Japanese defence posture. But if the US gets bogged down in a war with Saddam's forces, it will undermine US ability to deal with North Korea to the further detriment of Asian stability. For this reason, American allies in Asia can hardly afford to withhold support for the US over Iraq (including provision of logistics and overflight rights) while expecting it to take a firm stand on Pyongyang.

The contrasting US responses to Iraq and North Korea creates a difficult strategic dilemma for Asian states. American soft-handling of North Korea will undercut the legitimacy of its military campaign against Iraq, but outright confrontation with North Korea will not be without costs. It will alienate South Koreans who prefer a policy of dialogue and accommodation with the North. The recent wave of anti-Americanism in South Korea, fuelled by the non-conviction of two American soldiers blamed for the death of two Korean school girls, and implicitly backed by vested political interests in Seoul, makes it difficult for Seoul to support a hardline US posture against North Korea. This in turn is increasing anti-South Korea sentiments in the US Congress. One possible consequence of this could be to undermine domestic political support in the US for the current level of ground troop deployments in Korea. This would be seen as a dangerous development by US allies in the region who rely on a US-led regional balance of power for their security. The US may seek to compensate by increasing its long-range air and naval deployments in the Asia Pacific. America's allies, such as Singapore, may thus be called upon to offer greater access to US naval and air forces.

14

The War in Iraq: Morality or the National Interest?

The real debate about the war in Iraq is not between idealists (who oppose this war on moral grounds) and realists (who see wars as a normal and sometimes necessary feature of international order). It is between two schools of realists, with differing conceptions of the "national interest", judged in the context of the costs and benefits of the war in terms of its stated objectives outlined by the United States.

In defending its decision to launch the attack on Iraq, the Bush administration has offered three main justifications. The first is Iraq's suspected development of weapons of mass destruction. The second is Iraq's alleged link with terrorist groups, including the perpetrators of the September 11, 2001 attacks on the US. The third is the repression and misrule of the Iraqi people by the Saddam Hussein regime, which has reduced a once prosperous nation to ruin.

While the Bush administration's initial justification for the war related chiefly to the first two factors, during the final stages of preparation for the war, it stressed the third rationale. However, evidence is far from conclusive on the first justification while there is little evidence to support the second.

For those who take a moral stand against the war, it is the third reason which is the most difficult to argue against. Considering the brutality of the Saddam Hussein regime and the misery and damage it has inflicted on its own people, there is considerable justification for resort to armed intervention in Iraq to produce a regime change. The use of force to oust the Saddam Hussein regime and replace it with a more humane and democratic ruler could well recommend itself.

But such a war, idealists would argue, could only be justified under two conditions. First, it should be authorized by the UN. Second, it should be undertaken only after all other means, including diplomacy and containment, have been exhausted. Neither of the conditions was fulfilled before the current military campaign by US and allied forces began.

Not all idealists are against the use of force to achieve worthy collective objectives by the international community. Many in this camp are proponents of collective security (use of collective force to punish and repel aggression) and humanitarian intervention (use of force to punish dictators accused of gross violations of human rights). But for them, the current campaign against Iraq does not meet the criteria of collective security or a just war. More time should have been given to the weapons inspectors and more efforts made to achieve a compromise at the UN Security Council.

Yet, whether such actions as prescribed by the idealists would have led to Iraqi compliance is open to debate. The more powerful arguments against the war have come not from the idealists, but from those who think hard through the costs and benefits of unilateral military action in meeting the very objectives outlined by the war's proponents, especially the Bush administration. Realists from Sun Tzu to Hans Morgenthau had advised that national interests, especially in going into war, must be defined in terms of a cost-benefit analysis.

Hence, it is important to ask: will this war deter other countries from acquiring weapons of mass destruction? Not really, if North Korea's nuclear ambitions go unchecked. In fact, any further neglect of the North Korea crisis by the US will mean that the war against Saddam, including its "axis of evil" rationale, which stoked North Korean insecurity, would actually end up worsening the global proliferation problem. Will the war reduce the risk of international terrorism? Again, the answer is: not really. In fact, the opposite could happen, as the war provokes Muslim anger and adds fire to the terrorist ideology and recruitment.

Hence, one does not have to be a pacifist and join the anti-war demonstrations to realise the dangers created by this war. The risk of terror attacks on America and its allies has increased. There is every reason to think that the war will leave deep scars in the psyche of Muslim peoples which could destabilise pro-US regimes in the Middle East and elsewhere.

In this connection, the third professed US objective: the ouster of the Saddam dictatorship and its replacement by a popular regime as a step towards the eventual democratization of the Middle East, assumes importance. Rulers in the Middle East who have sided with the US could hardly welcome democratization really takes hold as a long-term goal of the US in the region. And many realists scholars and policymakers believe that democratization in the Third World is a prescription for greater conflict and disorder. Hence, in terms of its stated objectives, the current Gulf War does not vindicate the realist position and preferences about international order.

Nations backing the US in its war against Iraq have invoked the "national interest" to justify their position. This is entirely understandable. Both realists and moralists agree on the primacy of national interest. As President John F. Kennedy proclaimed in 1963, "every nation determines its policy in terms of its own interests".

Yet, national interest is a highly politicized and elastic notion subject to differing interpretations and manipulation. First, who defines what is national interest? Should it be the state exclusively or should it also take into account the views of various domestic groups, whether they are ethnic minorities, civic organizations, media, or even those protesting the war in the streets of London, Sydney and Manila? As Martha Finnemore, a political scientist at George Washington University, reminds us "much of international politics is about defining rather than defending national interests".

The meaning of national interest can vary widely, from increasing a state's power to the survival of a state to upholding international legitimacy. Many realists assume that national interests are mainly material, existing outside of perceptions. Yet, perceptions do matter, sometimes more than reality.

In the current war, if country X claims that its national interest is served by siding with the US, what does it really mean? It can mean that country X is so dependent on US military support (or US primacy and power more generally) that its national security would be undermined by opposing the US campaign and thereby prompting the US to cut-off its aid or withdraw its US security umbrella. Or national interest can mean that country X itself feels utterly vulnerable to terrorism and weapons of mass destruction, or some combination thereof, directly or indirectly (for example if such weapons fall into the hands of the terrorists in its own soil). Or national interest can mean that country X stands to gain increased US aid by offering political and logistical support to the US.

While many governments, enjoying a monopoly over defining the national interest, have invoked the concept, few have clarified to the international community and their people what exactly it is in this given crisis and which elements of the national interest are most important.

Is the loss of the credibility and effectiveness of the UN, however imperfect in the past, not damaging to the national interest of weak and vulnerable states, big or small? Will not the undermining of the Security Council's authority weaken the campaign to reduce the danger of proliferation of weapons of mass destruction? Will not the undermining of US moral authority, especially its image as a "benign superpower", damage the interests of those who have for decades relied on American military presence for their security and stability?

15

Fear, Power and Empire

The US attack on Iraq is best explained not as a product of national interest (a category which includes the desire for material gain), but as the result of an odd mixture of two other, apparently conflicting forces: fear and power. While most people describe the US policy in terms of the former, it is the other two factors, which are the main driving force behind this war.

Conventionally, wars are driven by threats, actual or perceived. The Bush administration has invoked two kinds of threats coming from Iraq: terrorism and weapons of mass destruction. Moreover, it has linked the two. But little evidence was presented before the war begun in support of either claim. If anything, it's a war in search of evidence rather than one based on evidence. Even then, evidence of Iraqi guilt in acquiring weapons of mass destruction (barring a possible chemical weapons programme) and supporting the September 11 terrorists is yet to be uncovered.

But to understand why the Bush administration has gone this far, one has to discard the conventional meaning of threat and instead focus on fear, a much more abstract, all encompassing, sometimes irrational and utterly subjective notion. September 11, 2001, ushered in what might be called a culture of fear in America.

While fear grips the whole world, it is most pronounced in the US, especially in the Bush administration. George W. Bush, the most powerful man on earth, also happens to be its most scared. In fact, power begets fear. The more powerful a nation is, the more fearful it becomes.

American politics and foreign policy under the Bush administration is increasingly being defined and driven by different kinds of fears: fear of Osama bin-Laden, fear of Saddam Hussein, fear of Islam, and fear of the United Nations and even fear of its own allies. As a result, international relations is now more about fear politics than power politics.

Moreover, the politics of fear has brought to the surface and fuelled a once incipient ideology of power. The United States has set out to impose its fears on others by pushing a vigorous ideology and agenda of power.

The present Gulf War is the most ideologically-minded conflict since the end of the Cold War. However, while Cold War produced just that, a Cold War, the current ideology produces hot wars and interventions, without being constrained by the kind of countervailing force that the former Soviet Union once provided. This ideology of power was clearly revealed at a recent gathering of the American Enterprise Institute. There, the chief ideologues of the Bush administration outlined their vision and agenda for the world, an agenda that included "radical reform of the United Nations, regime change in Iran and Syria, and 'containment' of France and Germany". They disdained the UN, whose time, according to Richard Perle, had "passed". The main goals of the US in the war, including the overthrow of Saddam and the democratic transformation of the Middle East, could all be achieved by the US alone, with no assistance from the UN.

Is this fear- and ideology-driven war legitimate? Here, it is important to distinguish legitimacy from legality. The legality of the war can be debated, while its legitimacy is far more suspect than its legality.

Moreover, it is important to distinguish legitimacy from morality. From a moral perspective, as I have argued elsewhere, the war against Saddam Hussein's brutal regime has a lot to recommend itself. But the Bush administration has made arguments based on American interests (including threat perceptions) not American morality. Many critics of the war, myself included, do not argue against the goal of removing the Saddam Hussein regime and its replacement with a just, humane and democratic ruler. But for them, the issue of legitimacy has to do with the means being employed, the timing of the war and the modality of its conduct.

The issue of legitimacy in modern wars is shaped by many factors. One key factor is international opinion, expressed through the public statements of leaders, peace rallies, direct or indirect action by national governments and parliaments and the total number of allies and collaborators that the chief warring nation could count on. By all these accounts, the American strike on Iraq falls short.

In the 1991 Gulf War, 30 coalition forces provided more than 295,000 troops to beef up a US force of 430,000. In the present Gulf

War, 47 countries have pledged to be a part of "the Coalition of the Willing". However, only 11 countries are directly contributing manpower to the war effort presently, and even then, most in a non-combat capacity. The main support to the US force of 255,000 troops comes from Britain, which has sent 45,000 troops, and Australia, which has deployed 2,000 troops.

Many of the nations, especially from Central Europe, which have joined the coalition of the willing, did not exist in 1991. In most cases, the coalition of the willing has been brought together because of its members' security dependence on the US or because of the carrot of US aid, as with many central European nations, who also have been offered NATO membership.

Security dependence is a key factor in the case of the support of South Korea and Japan for the war, both of whom have publicly admitted that support for the US is imperative in order to retain its military support against the escalating North Korean threat. Even then we are not sure what Japan's status is: One is not quite sure if Japan is listed under "the Coalition of the Willing"; according to some news reports, it is available for "post-conflict" support.

In the previous Gulf War, Japan and Germany paid the US$13 billion and US$5.5 billion respectively to subsidize its successful campaign to drive Saddam Hussein out of Kuwait. In this war, it is America which is doing the providing, and even then with mixed results. Witness Turkey's refusal to allow US forces passage through its territory in return for a hefty US$6 billion dollar aid package.

What is also striking is the rapidity with which the goodwill for the US generated by the September 11 attacks on the US has disappeared. To quote Jimmy Carter, a former US president, "The heartfelt sympathy and friendship offered to America after the 9/11 attacks, even from formerly antagonistic regimes, has been largely dissipated; increasingly unilateral and domineering policies have brought international trust in our country to its lowest level in memory".

Anti-war rallies have marked cities around the world: 30,000 in Washington DC on January 18; at least 750,000 people in London on February 15; one million in Rome; 660,000 in Madrid; 500,000 in Berlin; 100,000 in Paris. In New York, protesters stretched for 20 blocks along First Avenue and spilled west to Second Avenue. More than 100,000 people in San Francisco in the week of February 16. Between 30,000 and 50,000 protesters gathered in Sydney on March 23. During the week of 6 April, more than 100,000 people protested in strongly anti-war Germany, half of them at a rally in Berlin. During the week of March 29, 100,000 marched in Indonesia; 70,000 marched in Peshawar. And 30,000–50,000 workers in Seoul, protested their government's plan to support the US-led war effort by dispatching non-combat troops.

But the legitimacy of wars is not merely a function of public perceptions and opinion only. A good deal of current thinking on the legitimacy of wars comes from the so-called just war tradition, which subsumes adherence to collective security justifications and norms of ethical conduct in combat situations.

The just war tradition, which dates back to the period of St Augustine in the 4th century and St Thomas Aquinas in the 13th century, has two components. The first is *Jus ad bellum* (justice of a war). This combines several principles.

1. It must be a war of last resort.
2. It must be sanctioned by a legitimate authority (state or international organization).
3. It must be waged over a just cause: not aggression nor desire for revenge.
4. It must have a good chance of success; wars fought for good causes but which result in failure are not justified.
5. It must end in peace, and produce an outcome better than before.

The second component of just war theory is *Jus in bello* (justness of the manner in which the war is being fought). This has two main components.

1. The principle of proportionality: potential benefits from war must outweigh negatives such as destruction and death. Military force limited to level of violence required to achieve the mission; any risk to civilians must be proportionate to the military value of the target.

2. The principle that wars must be discriminate: combatants and non-combatants must be treated differently. Civilians must not be intentionally targeted. Civilian casualties must be minimal.

Among recent commentators, the former US President, Jimmy Carter has actually invoked the just war criteria. He argues that the current war falls short on several grounds. According to Carter, "clear alternatives to war" did exist. Moreover, Carter points to the lack of legitimate authority for the war. The Security Council's authorization which forms the administration's stated legal basis of the war was meant to eliminate Iraq's weapons of mass destruction, and not "achieve regime change and to establish a Pax Americana in the region, perhaps occupying the ethnically divided country for as long as a decade". For these objectives, Carter says, the US does not have international authority.

Indeed, not only does the war not have authority from the UN, it is also being conducted on an ideological platform which sees the UN as an antiquated dinosaur which has little place in the emerging world order.

Many other observers of the Middle East such as Carter are not convinced that the US attack on and occupation of Iraq will produce a clear improvement on the situation that exists now. "Although there are visions of peace and democracy in Iraq, it is quite possible that the aftermath of a military invasion will destabilise the region and prompt terrorists to further jeopardise our security at home. Also, by defying overwhelming world opposition, the United States will undermine the United Nations as a viable institution for world peace".

Let us look at *jus in bello* now, which says that the war's weapons must discriminate between combatants and non-combatants. How do we honour this dictum, despite best intentions? Extensive aerial bombardment, no matter how accurate, inevitably results in "collateral damage". While the US military has emphatically stated that it is avoiding targets which might house civilian population, this is difficult to ensure when many military targets happen to be near private homes, hospitals, mosques and schools. And thanks to the suicide attacks on US forces, the US military is less able to tell the terrorist from the civilian.

As regards proportionality, the Bush administration has not been able to prove a definitive link between the September 11 terrorist attacks and the Saddam Hussein regime, a link which would have made the US attack proportional to the September 11 attacks on the US.

I should stress here that the just war tradition is not just a Christian doctrine. Many of the same principles can be found in the Report of the International Commission on Humanitarian Intervention and State Sovereignty, entitled *Responsibility to Protect.*

No other policy document has gone further in specifying the criteria for humanitarian intervention. The Report sets down six specific and important conditions which can justify military action against a regime: just cause, right intention, last resort, proportional means and reasonable prospects and above all, right authority.

In defining "just cause" the Report argues that intervention, even to protect lives, is not justified unless it is meant to stop large-scale loss of life and ethnic cleansing or to protect their nationals in foreign territory. "Right intention" is similarly limited to alleviation of acute human suffering rather than alteration of boundaries or even supporting claims of self-determination. It excludes intervention to restore democracy in a country. Outright overthrow of oppressive regimes is not justified, unless they have engaged in large-scale killing and ethnic cleansing. In such cases, the report advocates containment and sanctions, aimed at destroying the ability of such regimes to cause harm to their own people.

Even so, the report argues, such intervention should only be a last resort, it should be proportional to the violations committed, it should have reasonable prospects for success, and most importantly, it should be authorised by the UN. This report represents the consensus view of both the North and the South, from all religions and civilizations. The current war in the Gulf would seem to violate most of the principles laid down in the *Responsibility to Protect.*

As I have argued elsewhere, "If intervention aimed at preventing large-scale loss of life and ethnic cleansing and undertaken through a legitimate multilateral framework is to be accepted only as an 'extreme', 'extraordinary' and 'exceptional' measure, shouldn't there be even less justification for the self-interested intervention by a single nation, no matter however powerful, motivated by its strategic and geopolitical objectives"?

Some would say that decisions and justification about wars should not be based on moral grounds such as the just war principles, but should instead focus on the national interest. The Bush administration has indeed done so. "It's in our national interest, as well, that we deal with Saddam Hussein", declared Bush at his White House Press Conference on March 6, 2003. For academic scholars, the meaning of national interest varies from ensuring survival to seeking international legitimacy. For this administration, however, national interest equates the unabashed pursuit of power.

This, of course, is nothing unexceptional. The influential scholar of international relations, Hans Morgenthau, defined national interest in essentially power terms and in a much early era, Greek historian Thucydides had proclaimed: "The strong get what they want and the weak suffer what they must".

Let us turn to who is defining the national interest in the US today and how is it being defined. It's clear that a small band of neo-conservative elite within the US has arrogated itself to an ideological pulpit from which it could define America's national interest. It is the William Kristols, Richard Perles and Paul Wolfowitzs. One is not sure whether the more moderate members of the Bush cabinet, such as Colin Powell, have a say in defining the national interest.

Goaded by this elite, the Bush administration follows a specific meaning of national interest defined as power in a way that the Athenians in Thucydides' Melian dialogue would have approved. Thus, in September 2002, a document called the "National Security Strategy of the United States" proclaimed that "the President has no intention of allowing any foreign power to catch up with the huge (military) lead the US has opened since the fall of the Soviet Union". Moreover, "Our forces will be strong enough to dissuade potential adversaries from pursuing a military build-up in hopes of surpassing, or equalling, the power of the US".

But a purely power-centric approach based on a narrowly defined conception of national-interest carries major costs. Power without legitimacy begets resistance and insecurity. While the Athenians destroyed the relatively weak island of Melos with considerable ease, they could not defend their empire for too long. As Thucydides noted in explaining the causes of the Pelopenesian War, it was the relentless rise of Athenian power and the fear it caused in Sparta and its neighbours that ultimately led to the war that destroyed Athenian hegemony. Thucydides—who believed war was the result of the breakdown of balance of power—was no idealist.

Of course, America is not an empire in the sense Athens once was. Yet, think-tank circles in Washington, DC are agog with the talk of an American empire. As Joseph Nye, dean of Harvard's Kennedy School of Government, recently pointed out, people in America "are now coming out of the closet on the word 'empire'".

Are we witnessing the beginning of an American empire based on the twin forces of fear and power? Many defenders of the Bush administration assert that the US has no desire or resources to create an imperial nation. A November 2002 article in the online version of the conservative Washington journal, *National Review*, by Victor David Hanson, entitled "A Funny Sort of Empire" took issue with the detractors of the nation who accuse it of having imperial designs. It offered several reasons why there cannot be an American empire similar to the old empires of Greece, Rome, or the European nations.

First, unlike the Athenians, Romans, Ottomans, and the British, America does not take land and treasure and annex territory. As Hanson points out, America hasn't taken anyone's soil since the Spanish-American War.

But some empires did rule indirectly and remained authentic empires. The British rule in Malaysia is a good example of this. And petroleum, also known as "black gold", is the real treasure of the modern era.

What about territory? Last year, in a new book entitled *The American Empire: The Realities and Consequences of American Diplomacy*, the author Andrew J. Bacevich wondered "whether the US can go on exercising hegemony by indirect means, or will be inexorably drawn into the business of direct imperial rule. For up to now, one of the reasons there has been so little real opposition to US hegemony in most of the world is precisely that this hegemony is distant and indirect".

With the planned occupation of Iraq, this is no longer a theoretical possibility. The reality of American empire is with us now. The question is not whether America will engage in direct rule, but whether the problems that came with territorial possession to the old empires will also come to bedevil the American empire.

Another factor working against an American empire is that American people and politicians have been, and remain basically isolationist: "The Athenian ekklesia, the Roman senate, and the British Parliament writes Hanson, alike were eager for empire and reflected the energy of their people. In contrast, America went to war late and reluctantly in World Wars I and II, and never finished the job in either Korea or Vietnam. We were likely to sigh in relief when we were kicked out of the Philippines, and really have no desire to return".

Yet, the American public has backed the war with the full knowledge that victory over Saddam Hussein will be followed by American rule over Iraq for some years to come. Moreover, the isolationist streak is clearly more true of the American public than its neo-conservative power elite. Given the opportunity, this gang would like to move America in the direction of empire, and has indeed said so in so many words. And if this particular elite hangs onto power for another four years, then it could set the course for a long-term policy that cannot be easily reversed. No one has said empires have to last forever.

A third argument against an American empire advanced by Hanson is that Americans have no culture of empire rooted in conceptions of personal glory, unlike the "desire of a young Roman quaestor or the British Victorians was to go abroad, shine in battle, and come home laden with spoils".

One answer to this may be simple: Have you seen Rambo?

More seriously, Hanson argues that America cannot have an empire when its defense spending is in decline. Hanson says that "America spends less of its GNP on defence than it did during the last five decades. And most of our military outlays go to training, salaries, and retirements—moneys that support, educate, and help people rather than simply stockpile weapons and hone killers. The eerie thing is not that we have 13 massive $5 billion carriers, but that we could easily produce and maintain 20 more".

But resources and spending are relative. Let me offer a quick look at the extent of US dominance of the world military power hierarchy. The US is the only country with nuclear and conventional forces that have a truly global reach. US military spending is higher than that of the next eight countries combined. The US leads the world in RMA (Revolution in Military Affairs) technology and weapon systems. The 31 per cent American share of the world product, in market prices, is equal to that of the next four countries combined (Japan, Germany, Britain and France).

Between 1985 and 2001, the US share of world defense spending increased—from 31 per cent to 39 per cent. (Its share of world spending is likely to surpass 42 per cent in 2003). Standing alone, the United States moved from spending only 80 per cent as much as the adversary group in 1985 to spending 250 per cent as much in 2001. Today the US accounts for almost 60 per cent of all military R&D spending worldwide.

A final point of contention about an American empire is not whether it is possible, but whether it won't be such a bad thing after all. Hanson argues that an American empire, if it is to come about at all, will not spread misery but freedom. "The Athenians killed, enslaved, exacted, and robbed on Samos and Melos. No one thought Rome was going into Numidia or Gaul—one million killed, another million enslaved—to implant local democracy. Nor did the British decide that at last 17th century India needed indigenous elections. But Americans have overthrown Noriega, Milosevic, and Mullah Omar and are about to rid Iraq of Saddam Hussein, to put in their places elected leaders, not legates or local client kings".

Sure enough. But the US has in the past also supported brutal dictatorships. As anyone with a faint knowledge of the history of the Cold War would know, there is a conspicuous record of American support for dictators and autocrats; Syngman Rhee in South Korea and Pinochet in Chile, the Somozas in Nicaragua to name just a few. And now there is Musharraf of Pakistan. And historical record shows that democracies are not easily imposed by foreign powers through the use of force.

In 1899, Elihu Root, the American Secretary of War, claimed: "the American soldier is different from all other soldiers of all other countries since the world began. He is the advance guard of liberty and justice, of law and order and of peace and happiness".

Yet, in the fog of battle in an Age of Fear, soldiers, American or otherwise, quickly lose their ability to distinguish between civilians and combatants. As we have seen in the days since the war began, every truck or car may appear as a potential suicide bomber.

Perhaps one might argue that America's imperial ambitions would be kept under check by its closest ally, Britain, who is also its predecessor as the global hegemon. But then one is reminded of the words of Harold McMillan, who while he was Minister at Allied Headquarters in North Africa in 1943, was supposed to have said: "These Americans represent the new Roman Empire—and we Britons, like the Greeks of old, must teach them how to make it go".

Sources

Andrew J. Bacevich, *The American Empire: The Realities and Consequences of American Diplomacy* (Cambridge, MA; Harvard University Press, 2002).

Dana Milbank and Mike Allen, "Bush Urges Commitment to Transform Mideast", *Washington Post*, November 7, 2003.

Carter, Timmy, "Principles of a just War London US Campaign", *New York Times*, March 16, 2003.

Janadas Devan, "Playing the Unwilling Enemy to the U.S.", *Straits Times*, March 28, 2003.

Joseph S. Nye, "Lessons in Imperialism", *Financial Times*, June 16, 2002.

Ken Simons, "Sovereignty and Responsibility to Protect".

National Security Strategy of United States of America, (The White House, September 2002).

Peace Magazine, Vol. 19, No. 1 (January/March 2003); Jimmy Carter, "This Will Not Be A Just War", *The Guardian* March 12, 2003.

"Toeing the Blue Line: Perspective on Peace Operations", *Journal of International Affairs*, Vol. 55, No. 2 (Spring 2002).

Victor David Hanson, "A Funny Sort of Empire: Are Americans Really So Imperial?" *National Review*, November 27, 2002.

16

Coalition of the Willing or Coalition of the Coaxed and Coerced?

While retaliating against Saddam Hussein for his invasion of Kuwait, George Herbert Walker Bush, the President of the United States, proclaimed in his January 1991 State of the Union address: "What is at stake is more than one small country, it is a big idea—a new world order, where diverse nations are drawn together in common cause to achieve the universal aspirations of mankind: peace and security, freedom, and the rule of law".

Now that the war in the Gulf waged by his son is almost over, what kind of vision for a world order could we expect him to announce? Bush may be wise to refrain from offering any grand and sweeping vision for a post-Saddam world, lest he be accountable for its realization. Perhaps he would be content to let the neo-conservatives of Washington do the talking about global reordering, something they had already done with gusto before the war and would do so now with the jubilation flowing from Saddam's defeat.

In fact one of them, Richard Perle, has just done that. Remarkably, he too invokes the phrase New World Order, but with an important twist. It's to be a "new world order that's up to the task". Bush Sr.'s New World Order was "an order in which a credible United Nations can use its peacekeeping role to fulfil the promise and vision of the United Nations' founders". In contrast, Perle's New World Order seeks to replace the UN with a "coalition of the willing" approach, of the kind that scored an overwhelming military victory over Saddam Hussein's forces without Security Council authorization.

According to Perle, "far from disparaging them [the coalition of the willing] as a threat to a new world order, we should recognize that they are, by default, the best hope for that order, and the true alternative to the anarchy caused by the dismal failure of the UN".

What do we make of the coalition of the willing idea? Two important caveats before we even discuss this idea. First, Richard Perle is not the Bush administration, although he until recently was a member of the Pentagon's Defense Policy Advisory Board. Second, the Bush administration is not America, and here I don't refer to Bush's narrow victory over Al Gore in the last presidential election. Bush may be a legitimate president, but presidents come and go in democratic America which remains a wellspring of alternative approaches to world order and where no particular flock of policy hawks can claim to define the "national interest". While Americans supported the war against Saddam in overwhelming numbers, it does not mean they support the foreign policy approach that Perle advocates.

But what about Perle's New World Order vision and the coalition of the willing agenda? Perle writes: "What died with the Security Council's unwillingness to sanction force to implement its own resolutions on Iraq's possession of weapons of mass destruction was the decades-old fantasy of the UN as the bedrock of world order". Many observers will contest this view and argue that the Security Council's "unwillingness" to authorize force was time-specific, rather than a total rejection of such a course of action, and that Iraq's possession of weapons of mass destruction had not been proven beyond reasonable doubt *before* the war was launched.

Moreover, "the decades-old fantasy" that Perle so disparages happened to be one shared by a succession of distinguished American leaders, from Franklin Roosevelt to Bill Clinton, and that even Jeanne Kirkpatrick, Bush Sr.'s ambassador to the UN, was described the 1991 Desert Storm operation as a demonstration of how a "reinvigorated United Nations could serve as a global policeman in the New World Order".

The concept of a coalition of the willing is nothing new and not by itself illegitimate. It has been tried by NATO in Kosovo (without UN authorization) and by an Australian-led force in East Timor (with prior UN authorization). In fact, Kofi Annan himself concedes that the world is better with such an option than without it when confronted with imminent tragedies such as the massacre of half a million people in Rwanda and Burundi or massive instances of ethnic cleaning as in the Balkans in the 1990s.

Generally, however, this notion of the coalition of the willing is meant to compliment the UN, and to compensate for its limitations in mobilizing resources and offering timely action. Its legitimacy rests on prior UN authorization, and failing that, at least a post-facto UN authorization. But regularising such an approach to deal with one's fears at the expense of the UN is something else. Will such an approach to world order prove more effective, if not legitimate? Let me highlight three major problems.

First, who will comprise this coalition of the willing? Look at the current Gulf war. Although there are no definitive numbers, one website (http://www.areporter.com/sys-tmpl/thecoalitionofthewilling/) lists 41 countries: Afghanistan; Albania; Australia; Azerbaijan; Bulgaria; Colombia; Costa Rica; Czech Rep.; Denmark; Dom. Rep.; El Salvador; Eritrea; Estonia; Ethiopia; Georgia; Honduras; Hungary; Iceland; Italy; Japan; South Korea; Latvia; Lithuania; Macedonia; Micronesia; Netherlands; Nicaragua; Palau; Philippines; Poland; Portugal; Romania; Slovakia; Spain; Solomon Isls.; Tonga; Turkey; Ukraine; UK; Uzbekistan; and USA. This is larger than the 34-member coalition which fought Saddam in 1991. But while that coalition, as a *Washington Post* report of March 25, 2003 pointed out, was "an actual military coalition, with all members providing troops, aircraft, ships or medics", only seven members of the present coalition were listed as providing combat troops (including 45,000 from Britain and 2,000 from Australia and one submarine and one warship from Denmark), with another seven offering other forms of support, such as decontamination experts, medical ships, non-combat troops and troops for post-war deployment. Moreover, six members of the 23 March list are unarmed nations: Palau, Costa Rica, Iceland, the Marshall Islands, Micronesia and the Solomon Islands. Absent from the coalition are countries such as Canada, Germany, and India.

Moreover, the 2003 group is not so much a Coalition of the Willing, as a coalition of the coerced. At the 1991 Gulf War, the US asked for and received several billion dollars from its allies, especially Germany and Japan. Now the billions have flowed in the opposite direction so far (unless there have been secrete donations). Turkey was offered US$6 billion in aid to permit its territory to be used as an invasion route to Iraq, although it refused the offer. Many members of the 2003 coalition were coaxed by prospects for US aid and other benefits, such as NATO membership, while others joined because of their acute security dependence on the US. This dependence ranges from Micronesia, which is by treaty totally dependent on the US for its defence, to South Korea, whose decision to join the coalition cannot be unrelated to fears created by revelations about North Korea's nuclear weapons programme (itself linked to the Bush doctrine of pre-emption), and the Philippines, which is acutely dependent on US support for its war against terror in the southern Philippines.

If the world is to accept a coalition of the willing as an alternative to the UN, will the US allow the same right to other nations and regional organizations to form their own coalitions of the willing to carry out interventions in their backyard?

Consider a not-so-hypothetical case. Senior Cabinet ministers of India have in the past week are argued that Pakistan is a deserving target of pre-emption because it meets the three criteria laid down by the Bush Doctrine: an authoritarian regime, which possesses and exports (to North Korea) weapons of mass destruction, and harbours terrorists which carry out attacks against India. What if India puts together a coalition of the willing comprising Israel, Iran, and some other nations to attack and destroy the nuclear facilities of Pakistan? Shouldn't this be considered as a legal act, unless Perle's concept is limited to coalitions developed and controlled by the United States alone?

17

Debating the Gulf War

The recently-concluded Gulf War has proven to be a highly divisive affair in international relations. It has polarised the trans-Atlantic community, created new fissures between the Muslim and non-Muslim societies, and divided academic analysts.

Critics of the Bush administration's decision to go to war against Iraq without UN authorization have recently themselves come under much criticism. They are accused of ignoring the liberation of the long-oppressed oppressed Iraqi people that the war produced. Earlier, they were accused of ignoring the threat posed by Iraq's weapons of mass destruction. Some dissenting states are also being "punished" by the Bush administration for their alleged anti-Americanism. Dissenting columnists and writers in America and abroad have been subjected to hate-mail.

To make sense of the debate, it is important to appreciate the many differences in the positions taken by the war's critics. The war had indeed made strange bedfellows. It brought together traditional conservatives (not to be confused with the "neo-cons") like Pat Buchanan, perennial America critic Noam Chomsky, international political theorists John Mearsheimer and Stephen Walt, economist Paul Krugman, former President and Nobel Peace Prize winner Jimmy Carter, and British Labour politician Robin Cook.

While all opposed the war, they did so for different reasons. Some had a reflexive antipathy towards American hegemony. Others based their position on considered judgements about the war's stated rationale, and its implications for international order and American leadership.

First, there are those on the far right of the American political spectrum who opposed the war because they are deeply suspicious of America's global engagement as part of an internationalist agenda. Pat Buchanan belongs here.

Another group opposed the war on outright moral grounds: it did not meet the principles of "just war" such as whether there was sufficient provocation for the war, whether the means employed were proportionate to the offense caused and whether the war offered enough protection to civilians.

A third group consists of academics John Mersheimer and Stephen Walt, the leading exponents of political realism in the pantheon of American international relations scholars. They called this an "unnecessary war" because the threat that Saddam posed was not something that could not have been checked through a policy of "containment".

A fourth group of war critics were simply upset by what they saw as the Bush administration's false rationale for the war. Paul Krugman has attacked "a pattern of loud assertions and muted or suppressed retractions" which the Bush administration indulged in over evidence concerning Iraq's alleged possession of weapons of mass destruction.

A fifth group saw the war as an example of the gross inequities of the current international order, where the strong get what they want and the weak suffer what they must. Mahathir Mohammad of Malaysia is a good source for memorable quotes in this line of attack; his critique also reflected, like that of many others in the Muslim world mindful of domestic sensitivities, frustration and anger over the US support for Israel and what they see as an anti-Muslim agenda in the US foreign policy.

Finally, opposition to the war came from those who would have supported military action against Saddam but only after giving the UN inspectors more time, which might also have given the Security Council more time to strike a compromise. For this group, the costs of war in terms of the divisions created and the loss of credibility of the UN outweighed the benefits that came from the ouster of Saddam, especially in the absence of solid proof of his possession of dangerous weapons and sponsorship of terrorism.

It is also important to bear in mind that the supporters of the war were also acting out of diverse interests. Some like Australia backed America out of traditional alliance commitments, others, like many East European governments, were mindful of the security and material rewards of backing America. Some supporters of the war also had to worry about America's retaliation which could follow their withholding of support at this critical juncture. Another reason for supporting the US was the concern that letting Saddam to stay in power would have severely undermined American credibility and encourage other dictators to challenge global and regional stability. A few states were genuinely worried about the threat posed by Iraq's potential to develop weapons of mass destruction.

The suffering of the Iraqi people under Saddam's dictatorship came to be another reason to support the US in the final lead-up to the war. But whether this was a genuine concern or a convenient (but entirely legitimate) excuse can be debated. There are three reasons for scepticism. First, as Bush's spokesman Ari Fleischer, noted on April 11, 2003, Iraq's weapons of mass destruction "is what this war was and is about". Second, Saddam's tyranny did not appear overnight. Third, not all the supporters of the war endorse the emerging doctrine of humanitarian intervention, which calls for military action intervention to save peoples from oppression by their own rulers.

On the contrary, this doctrine, endorsed by the Senior Bush administration in Somalia and Clinton in Kosovo, has been and would continue to be seen by many supporters of the Iraq War as an unwelcome threat to state sovereignty. Yet, disagreement with the war's rationale has come from some of the staunchest supporters of humanitarian intervention, such as France, which opposed the war, and Canada, which stayed out of the coalition of the willing.

Those criticizing the war were by no means endorsing the Saddam regime. If the Bush administration is to make protection of human rights from oppressive regimes through military intervention the main plank of its foreign policy, then it will find support from at least some people and governments who opposed the Iraq war.

Neither were the critics of the war rejecting American values or dismissing its past contribution to international and regional order. Indeed, it's the opposite concern that might have motivated some of the war's critics: that the values and approaches which were pioneered by America for the great good of humankind were put at some risk by the way the action over Iraq unfolded. Take, for example, the institution of multilateralism. John Ruggie, a leading scholar on international institutions now at Harvard's Kennedy School, once wrote that the emergence of multilateralism in world affairs was not a by-product of American *hegemony*, but of *American* hegemony. It emerged essentially as a projection of fundamental American values and liberal domestic institutions onto the world stage. Hence, it would be especially ironic if people who question America's retreat from mutlilateralism are to be labelled as "anti-American".

What is clear is that many critics of the war from within and outside the US remain believers in fundamental American values and approaches to international order, just as many supporters of the war would not endorse American policies and preferences in all areas of international relations.

A meaningful debate about the war can only be based on a recognition of this complexity. Lumping all disagreements with the Iraq war's rationale and timing as "anti-American" would be simplistic and possibly dangerous, as it would futher the perception of growing "anti-Americanism" around the world that the wannabe-Osamas and Saddams, the real foes of America, would dearly love to encourage and exploit.

18

How Will Mr. Bush Run the World?

The post-Cold War international order collapsed the day American forces stormed Baghdad to put an end to the Saddam Hussein regime despite Washington's lack of authorization from the United Nations. While debate over who is to blame for its demise and whether it could have been preserved with more time and sincere effort will be a useful academic pastime, it's really time now for sober reflection on what kind of new order is emerging. Two questions are important for policymakers in Asia and around the world. First, what is the new American approach to international security? Second, are we witnessing a paradigm shift in America's foreign policy framework?

The goals of the Bush international order are not simply the old-fashioned geopolitical agenda of securing foreign bases and resources. Although these remain important, the Bush agenda is dominated by new fears: of tyrants, terrorists and weapons of mass destruction (WMD), and some combination of these. And its responses to these fears are conditioned by important changes in the American psyche brought about by the September 11 terrorist attacks, which have put paid to the post-Vietnam aversion to foreign military engagements that carry the risk of American casualties.

Some aspects of the Bush foreign policy agenda aspire to a moral clarity that the neo-conservatives close to the administration have long advocated and demanded. For them, the lines in the emerging international order are drawn clearly between an "Axis of Evil" on the one hand and an "Empire of the Good" on the other. Regime change occupies an important place in this agenda. This was confirmed by President George W. Bush himself in his April 16 speech at St Louis: "In this new era of warfare, we can target a regime, not a nation. Our aim is to track and strike the guilty. Terrorists and tyrants have now been put on notice. They can no longer feel safe hiding behind innocent lives".

The reality may not be so simple and stark, however. While the Bush team's aim is to make the US safe from tyrants, those who seek WMD and those who sponsor international terrorists will remain important, it will face several reality checks. For example, regime change in North Korea through military intervention may not be worth the risk or it has to be attempted differently from the Iraq way. One has to be careful about generalizing from the Iraq episode about how the US will respond to other, apparently similar, challenges.

Similarly, for political and economic reasons, the US will not reject international cooperation in every instance, although the appeal of the UN to a serving US president is clearly at its lowest point in memory.

But what seems evident is that in managing its own vision of international order, the Bush administration will seek to employ several new instruments. Three are especially important:

1. Pre-emptive military strikes. To some observers, the war has vindicated the Bush doctrine of pre-emption. It is unlikely that pre-emption will become unexceptional in the US approach to rogue states. But there are indications that others might emulate the American pre-emptive approach with their own local variations. Japan, Australia and India have each indicated that pre-emption is at least one of the options in dealing with neighbours.

2. Using "Coalitions of the Willing" to replace standing alliances and multilateral organizations. Neo-conservative Richard Perle has mounted a vigorous defence of this approach and called for regularising it. Some Europeans also seem to be building their own such coalition. Already, four European nations have announced a plan to create a joint force to act in crisis. If developed as a full-fledged instrument, this would enhance European autonomy and further weaken the North Atlantic Treaty Organisation (NATO), already reeling from transatlantic rifts over Iraq.

3. A system of rewards and punishments. This is evident from the way the Bush administration is treating its coalition partners and critics. The punishments range from diplomatic snubs to France, Germany and Canada, to the possible delaying of a free trade deal with Chile. The rewards meted out so far include Iraq contracts for British companies, and the import of Philippine workers to rebuild Iraq.

While these changes are important, whether they amount to a paradigm shift is another matter. Some of these new instruments reflect America's sheer military prowess. Here, the US remains and will continue to remain essentially unchallenged. But long-term change in the US strategic outlook and approach also depends on at least five factors:

1. Whether the neo-cons will function as a cohesive influence and how long they will last. The influence of neo-cons over Bush policy could be exaggerated. Moreover, their sweeping agenda of an American-imposed international order may in reality be a more restricted wish to ensure the security of Israel—a goal which seems to have been largely accomplished by the war (with US forces entrenched in Iraqi bases and exercising a coercive influence on Syria, the only remaining Middle East power capable of threatening Israel).

2. The state of the American economy. The key issue here is not whether the US can afford the cost of the war and rebuilding Iraq. Iraqi reconstruction can be financed from its oil revenues. But the US economy is facing serious challenges not necessarily related to the war. These include the prospects of a recession; there has been large-scale unemployment and the Dow Jones Industrial Average has declined by a quarter since January 2001. A recession-hit economy will make it difficult for Mr. Bush to sustain increased defence spending and finance new foreign ventures to implement the Bush Doctrine.

3. The severity of the terrorist threat. Mr. Bush was able to sell the war to the American people by linking Iraq with the September 11 attacks. Some analysts feel that the global terrorist threat after September 11 was overstated. Moreover, measures to suppress and defeat terrorism, undertaken both at the national and international levels, were already bearing fruit before the Iraq War. The threat of terrorist attacks has not disappeared, but if it declines further—a big "if" here—this will undermine the rationale and domestic support in the US for the Bush Doctrine.

4. How long will it take for the US to accept rapprochement with Old Europe? Some critics of the war, such as Germany, have shown signs of moving closer to the British position of trying to restrain US unilateralism from inside the camp, rather than from outside. If the US responds positively to these overtures, it may have to pay greater heed to Europe's interest in keeping the multilateral system alive. A continuing rift with Europe would add to the rationale for US policies that undermine the multilateral system.

5. Alternatives from within America. Americans have a long history of alternative approaches to world order. Ronald Reagan's "evil empire" rhetoric gave way to George Bush Sr.'s "New World Order". This time, the turn to neo-Reaganism could permeate think-tank, media and academic circles for a while.

But there is always the possibility of change. Liberal America, which champions multilateralism and diplomacy over force, is now keeping a low profile against neo-con forces in the US media (the Fox network), think-tank circles (American Enterprise Institute) and Mr Bush's own popularity. But they are far from defeated yet.

19

Coping with American Power

The quick and overwhelming victory of the US over the Saddam Hussein regime was hardly an unexpected outcome, despite momentary doubts about the strategy in the early days of the war. But what remains really uncertain now is how the US will use its post-war clout to create and manage international and regional order. The US approach will vitally shape the stability of Asia.

As is the case in all major wars, this Gulf War is having a mixed impact on international and Asian security. On the positive side, it has prompted North Korea to take a more moderate posture: a shift from brinkmanship to diplomacy. This is a welcome development for Japan, South Korea, China and the rest of the region. On the other hand, the war has consequences which, if unchecked, could be destabilizing. First, it strengthens pre-emption as a strategic doctrine. It adds weight to the case made by some Japanese officials about pre-emptive strikes against North Korea should the latter's nuclear and missile programme threaten Japanese security. There is a good reason to believe that the benefits of a pre-emptive strategy in deterring terrorist threats and rogue states are outweighed by negative consequences of unilateral pre-emption for deterrence and strategic stability.

Another negative consequence is the division of Asian opinion, both public and official, about the war. Japan, Philippines, South Korea and Singapore officially joined the US-led "coalition of the willing", although none provided combat troops to the operation like Australia. Malaysia and Indonesia remained critical, sometimes harshly, about the US attack.

But to keep the region from being polarized into a pro-US and anti-US camp, these intra-Asian differences need to be managed. Otherwise, a casualty could be Asia-Pacific regional institutions involving the US and its close ally, Australia (whose image had suffered before its strong support for the US invasion due to the Howard Government's own talk about pre-emption against terrorist targets in neighbouring countries). The decline of Asia Pacific multilateralism might give a boost to East Asian cooperation, but there could be a fallout here as well if China perceives Japan's and Philippine's backing for the US as part of a long-term strategy to constrain Chinese power.

The war reconfirms US hegemony as the main driving force of international order. The military side of this was never in doubt. The key question now is how this hegemony will be exercised politically and diplomatically in addressing specific challenges that Asia faces. How would the US, which some have characterized as a neo-imperial power, exercise its political rule?

Since the end of World War II, the US shaped international order through a mix of power politics and multilateralism born out of enlightened self-interest. In Asia, the US provided public goods, including access to its markets and investments in the region and offered a security umbrella through a forward military presence and a network of alliances. Thus posture was credited by many as the basis of regional stability and growth for a good part of the Cold War period. While the US did not promote a regional multilateralism after WWII, the creation of the ASEAN Regional Forum (ARF) in 1994 with Japanese and ASEAN initiative filled this gap. The US, after some hesitancy did join this group and worked to strengthen it.

Some elements of the old approach will survive the war. But the gap between US power and those of its allies as well as adversaries has increased dramatically. Sections of the Bush administration view alliances as messy and unnecessarily constraining when it comes to military operations. Even where the US seeks the help of allies, the latter's role and influence over joint operations would be limited because they cannot keep up with US technical prowess. America's Asian alliances, always unequal entities, are more so now than before.

This is not to say that the US would choose a unilateral stance on Asian security issues in every instance and against every potential adversary in Asia. Indeed, a major irony of the current US unilateralism is its explicit call for multilateral approaches to the North Korean crisis. As the White House recently stated, in dealing with the Korean crisis, it would be "working in a multilateral fashion with our friends and allies. We believe this is a regional issue, not a bilateral issue. And we will continue to treat it as such." But it is important to bear in mind that the multilateral approach that the US seeks in the

Korean crisis is that of a small and ad hoc group, not the larger and more institutionalized ASEAN Regional Forum.

After Iraq, there will be a temptation on the part of the US (as suggested in some of the belligerent post-war statements towards Syria) to intimidate adversaries into compliance and submission by injecting the fear of overwhelming US power. For Asian countries who are not necessarily adversaries of Washington, one worry should be about how the US deals with dissenting voices. In the past, the US has handsomely rewarded countries which sided with its ideological crusades while ignoring or tolerating the views of those who expressed genuine and often philosophical disagreements with US policy and actions. Now the question arises: while targeting rogue states, will the US react harshly against allies or neutral nations who, whether for domestic reasons or out of deference to moral convictions, dare to offer genuinely dissenting voices. This will be a key test of the American-led security order in Asia.

Politics and Principles in the Age of Fear

"Freedom and fear are at war....I will not relent in waging this struggle for freedom and security for the American people".

President George W. Bush, Address to a Joint Session of Congress and the American People, September 20, 2001

"We will, for example, accept more annoying security checks. But we must also be careful to avoid violating our rights in the name of searching out terrorists. After all, if there is any logic in attacks like those on the World Trade Center and the Pentagon where no one claims responsibility, it is precisely in wanting us to overreact and undermine our core values."

Stansfield Turner, Talk at the Centre for International and Seniority Studies, Maryland School of Public Affairs, September 30, 2001

20

Terrorism and Democracy

Politics, not geopolitics or culture, may ultimately determine how the September 11 attacks and the American response to it reshape world order in the early 21st century. Many see these events as ushering in a clash of civilizations, or at least a renewed power rivalry among nations. But September 11 may exert its most profound impact on the relationship between states and societies, where a new struggle for legitimacy and authority looms, whether in Muslim or non-Muslim worlds. While September 11 produced some changes in inter-state and inter-civilizational relations, they pale in comparison with its roots in, and effects (and potential effects) on, state-society relations. Several signposts of this have emerged.

The first is the divergent perception of, and reactions to, September 11, on the part of governments and peoples. Throughout the Islamic world, including Saudi Arabia, Malaysia, Pakistan and Indonesia, societies showed less sympathy and support for the US than did their own governments. And a lot of this popular anger is directed against their own governments, especially those who had sided with the US or had not been sufficiently forthcoming in condemning the US military action in Afghanistan. Popular resentment of American support for Israel made it difficult, though not impossible, for their governments to show understanding and support for the US. President Megawati of Indonesia made a much publicized visit to the White House to show solidarity with the US. But domestic disapproval of this stance soon forced her to criticize the US attack on Afghanistan. Domestic pressures also explain why Prime Minister Mahathir of Malaysia, after making it difficult for his own citizens to travel to Afghanistan to fight with the Taliban, also attacked the US military campaign in Afghanistan. The war against terror is thus more divisive when it comes to the relationship between governments and their subjects than that between governments.

The perpetrators of September 11 were inspired as much by a hatred of their own governments as of American hegemony. Osama bin Laden's turn to full-blown mass terrorism was sparked by his well-known dislike of America but also of the autocratic ways of the Saudi royal family. Mohammed Atta, the apparent ring-leader of the September 11 terrorists, has been described by his German friends as having spoken with "increasing bitterness about what he saw as the autocratic government of President Hosni Mubarak and the small coterie of former army officers and rich Egyptians gathered around Mr Mubarak". Anti-Americanism of the kind that breeds the bin-Ladens of the world goes hand in hand with authoritarianism in the Middle East, where governments routinely permit their media to fuel anti-American sentiments so as to deflect attention from their own repressive rule. In this sense, America's war on terrorism, as Ellen Amster reminds us, is in reality one in which Washington is interposing in a fight between Islamic radicals and Arab governments.

The nexus between terrorism and authoritarianism has been a matter of some debate in Asia, and is an important aspect of the changing state-society relationship in the post-September 11 era. In the past, the debate about democracy was about whether democracy is good for development, and whether democratic transitions (as in Indonesia) are a catalyst for regional disorder. The debate on democracy in Asia after September 11 is about two questions; whether lack of democracy is a "root cause" of terrorism, and whether democracy limits the ability of states to effectively respond to it.

On the first question, Anwar Ibrahim, the deposed and jailed Deputy Prime Minister of Malaysia, has observed: "Osama bin-Laden and his protégés are the children of desperation; they come from countries where political struggle through peaceful means is futile. In many Muslim countries, political dissent is simply illegal." Anwar sees himself as a victim of authoritarian rule in Malaysia, and his comments reflect unresolved domestic struggles in Malaysia. The issue of terrorism and democracy come together in Malaysia; its government faces ongoing demands for political liberalisation while responding to a serious challenge from homegrown and Afghanistan-trained terrorists. Farish Noor, a Malaysian scholar of Islam, makes a direct link between terrorism and authoritarian politics in Malaysia:

> It is the absence of ... democratic culture and practices in the Muslim world in general ... that leads to the rise of self-proclaimed leaders like the Mullahs of Taliban, Osama bin laden and our own Mullahs

> and Osama-wannabes here in Malaysia. And as long as a sense of political awareness and understanding of democracy is not instilled in the hearts and minds of ordinary Muslims the world over ... we will all remain hostage to a bunch of bigoted fanatics who claim to speak, act and think on our behalf without us knowing so.

If the absence of democracy breeds terrorism, can democracy pre-empt and defeat the terrorist challenge? Some advocates of democracy in the Muslim world hope that "With more democracy ... and a stronger voice for advocates of democracy, popular frustrations are less likely to be misdirected, and the resort to violence and terror reduced, particularly among an increasingly disaffected and vulnerable young population". In Southeast Asia, Surin Pitswuan, a former Foreign Minister of Thailand who is a Muslim and who has been a leading voice for democracy in Southeast Asia, argues that democracy reduces the danger of terrorism by enhancing the conditions for inter-ethnic harmony in plural societies. "As we pursue our aspirations of democracy", he contends, "we know that we shall be free to practise our faith fully and on an equal basis with others who also have their own religious faith and rituals sacred to them".

But critics of democracy are unlikely to be convinced by the logic of such arguments. As the cases of the US, Israel and India demonstrate, democratic governance does not make a country immune to transnational terrorism. Thomas Homer-Dixon argues that the advanced industrial nations of the West are uniquely vulnerable to terrorism because of their growing complexity and interconnectedness, and their tendency to concentrate vital infrastructure in small geographic clusters. The fact that these nations also tend to be democracies is not inconsequential, since democracies are also theoretically restricted in their ability to conduct the kind of arbitrary detention and coercive investigation needed to prevent acts of terrorism.

But in supposedly "mature" democracies, such restrictions may be withering, as governments wake up to the dangers caused by traditional pitfalls of civil liberties in combating terror. This was demonstrated by the case of Zacarias Moussaoui, a French national, whose laptop computer—presumably with information about the impending September 11 attacks—could not be legally seized by the

US authorities in time to save the World Trade Center. Ironically, it is the immature new democracies, such as Indonesia and the Philippines, which may now be more vulnerable to terrorism because of their inability to imitate Ashcroft's America.

Democratization has not made countries such as Indonesia and the Philippines less prone to terrorist conspiracies and attacks, whether from within or without (both being interlinked in most cases). But they also offer the least defence against terror in a region where the main weapon against the terrorists has been the Internal Security Act, a holdover from colonial days which has been used to silence political opponents as effectively as religious fanatics. Indonesia's inability to replicate the efforts of its neighbours, Malaysia and Singapore, in suppressing suspected terrorists has been blamed on democratization (apart from the rise of Islam as a political force since the late Suharto period, and the various other kinds of ongoing domestic violence that make Indonesians relatively impervious to terrorism of the bin-Laden kind). After repealing the notorious Anti-Subversion Law of the Suharto era, Indonesia under its new democratic constitution does not provide for an Internal Security Act similar to those of its two neighbours. In the Philippines, President Arroyo has walked a political minefield and risked substantial domestic discontent in soliciting American help in her own war against terrorism even though the public is generally unsympathetic to the militant's cause.

The response of Southeast Asian governments to terrorism provides ammunition to those who see democratization as part of the problem, rather than solution, in confronting the terrorist challenge. For these critics, the case for democratization is undermined when one compares the responses of Malaysia and Singapore (with swift detention under the ISA) with that of Indonesia and the Philippines. "While it may be true that democracy might provide a long-lasting solution", writes Irman Lanti, an Indonesian scholar, "certainly democratization (as a process) might not, especially if it is conducted without clear agenda and planning ... What best can be done ... is opening up of political space for the society to engage in discussion with the state on various issues within the framework of the existing system. An ambitious project of democratizing these nations might further complicate the already complex problems there".

With democracy on the defensive (perhaps temporarily, only time will tell) in the debates about the causes of, and responses to, terrorism, who is to prevent governments from using national security as a camouflage for regime survival? By creating a sense of national unity and purpose, however brief and superficial, the war against terrorism, like any wars, presents governments with an opportunity to out-manoeuver their political opponents. This might be happening in Malaysia today. The war against terrorism thus easily translates into a war against freedom.

In the post-September 11 world, terrorism is rapidly emerging as a convenient and overarching label under which governments and academic analysts could lump any and all kinds of challenges to state authority and regime security. Self-determination, the much vaunted norm of the post-Cold War global political order, becomes a major casualty in this altered political and intellectual climate. Witness the haste with which Chinese official commentators, while showing some empathy for the US after September 11, demanded American understanding of China's own brush with "terrorism and separatism" in Xinjiang, Tibet and Taiwan, even though the Tibetans and Taiwanese have no record of terrorism. Already, months before September 11, the Shanghai Co-operation Organization (SCO), a regional grouping of China, Russia, Kazakhstan, Kyrgyzstan, Tajikstan and Ujbekistan, had issued a joint declaration of its defence ministers pledging "real interaction of the armed forces and other power structures of their countries in the fight against terrorism, separatism, and extremism." To be sure, terrorism and self-determination are not always separable. But in the absence of a common understanding of what terrorism means, governments can be expected to conflate terrorism and separatism to crush legitimate demands for self-determination, even the terror-free variety. Where terrorist acts are carried out in the name of self-determination, governments now have less reason to separate the tactics from the cause. Who tells the nations belonging to the global anti-terror alliance that their fight against a tactic (terrorism) must not come at the expense of a willingness to address the cause (demands for self-determination)?

The post-September 11 world order has suddenly become less hospitable for human rights around the world. An America which carries out secret detentions of legal and illegal aliens suspected of terrorism and imposes a blanket denial of Geneva convention rights on its Afghan prisoners in Cuba, loses its moral high ground as an advocate for human rights and democracy in the world. This message is unlikely to be lost on Asian governments, especially those who have accused the US of double standards when it comes to promoting human rights and democracy. They would feel even less constrained (if they ever were) in challenging the universality of human rights norms, especially when their domestic stability is at stake. This compounds another possible consequence of September 11, the decreased space for civil society, as discoveries are made of how some terrorist organizations thrived by claiming NGO status and adopting their modus operandi.

Last but not least, state-society relations post-September 11 will be challenged by the inevitable redefinition of "security". Before September 11, the security agenda of nations was reorienting towards "non-conventional" issues, e.g., environment, refugees, migration and abuse of human rights, etc. The paradigm of human security, or security for the people, had emerged as an alternative to national security, or security for states (and in real terms, regimes). But the distinction between national security and regime security, always tenuous, will now be further blurred. Transnational terrorism may well be classified as a non-conventional threat, but responding to this menace is very much spearheaded by conventional configurations of states. And with a vengeance, states everywhere are striking back and re-powering themselves against societal forces. They are doing so in a variety of ways, by regulating financial flows with a view to curb the economic lifeline of terrorist networks, tightening immigration controls, and remilitarizing borders. The US-Canadian border is no longer undefended. The power balance between globalization and government has shifted in favour of government.

Security is changing in another and more fundamentally ironic manner. The "traditional division of security threats into external and internal threats", declared Defence Minister Tony Tan of Singapore in the aftermath of September 11, "no longer held". The

American model of "homeland security" is finding roots in Asia and the world. Though ostensibly geared to defeating the terrorist menace, homeland security is also a highly elastic notion that could be made to cover all aspects of fighting "low-intensity" threats and controlling day-to-day lives. Going by the thinking of America's leading experts on future wars, the real heroes in the coming war on terrorism would not be the "Daisy-cutters" and "Predators" of Afghanistan, but the "pervasive sensors" found in America and its fellow-travelling nations, sensors which could be "attached to every appliance in your house, and to every vending machine on every street corner, and which would then register "your presence in every restaurant and department store".

In projecting the growing sense of insecurity within America, homeland security blurs the once fashionable distinction between Western and Third World security approaches, in which the latter focused on their domestic front while the former pursued defence against foreign military aggression. With Americans on American soil made to feel and act more insecure than their counterparts in India and Malaysia, the home front against terrorism has brought America's security predicament closer to that of the Third World. As both situations converge, it is well to remember the words of David Ignatius, "*But security is different. Like life itself, it is something for which people will pay almost any price*".

Sources

Anwar Ibrahim, "Growth of Democracy Is the Answer to Terrorism", *International Herald Tribune*, October 11, 2001.

Ellen Amster, "The Attacks Were a Bid for Power in the Arab World", *International Herald Tribune*, September 18, 2001, p. 10.

Ellen Amster, "The Attacks Were a Bid for Power in the Arab World", *International Herald Tribune*, September 18, 2001, p. 10.

http://www.puaf.umd.edu/CISSM/Publications/TurneronTerrorism.htm.

Neil MacFarquhar, "In Cairo, Father Defends Son as Too 'Decent' to be Hijacker", *International Herald Tribune*, September 20, 2001, p. 3.

Shaha Aliriza and Laila Hamad, "A Time to Help Mideast Democracts", *International Herald Tribune*, October 20–21, 2001, p. 6.

"Shanghai Forum Ready to Fight Terrorism, Separatism and Extremism", *Pravda* (On-line English edition), May 15, 2001. http://english.pravda.ru/world/2001/06/15/7789.html.

Straits Times, November 5, 2001.

David Ignatius, "Pervasive Sensors Can Net bin Laden", *International Herald Tribune*, November 12, 2001, p. 8.

Surin Pitswuan, "Islam in Southeast Asia: A Personal Viewpoint", *The Nation*, September 22, 2001.

"The Home Front: Security and Liberty", Editorial, *New York Times*, September 23, 2001, p. 16.

Thomas Homer-Dixon, "The Rise of Complex Terrorism", *Foreign Policy*, (January 2002).

Irman Lanti, personal communication, January 31, 2002.

21

The Retreat of History?

The war on terror waged by the United States challenges the thesis proposed by Francis Fukuyama that the end of the Cold War leaves liberal democracy and the free market as endpoints of history. Indeed, it suggests that they are in retreat.

Until now, the main criticism of Fukuyama has come from those who believe that alternatives to liberal democracy already exist or could emerge, for example, from non-Western civilizations, such as those influenced heavily by Confucianism or Islam. Indeed, an intense competition for ideas and political institutions was predicted in Samuel Huntington's thesis about the clash of civilizations, which challenged Fukuyama's end of history argument in one of the great debates of the post-Cold War era.

Fukuyama has vigorously defended his position in the light of developments since the terrorist attacks on the United States just over a year ago. In an article in the *Guardian* on October 11, he argued that radical Islam constitutes no serious alternative to Western liberal democracy. "Modernity is a very powerful freight train that will not be derailed by recent events," he wrote. "Democracy and free markets will continue to expand as the dominant organizing principles for much of the world". "We remain at the end of history because there is only one system that will continue to dominate world politics, that of the liberal-democratic West", Fukuyama stressed.

But in the post-post-Cold War era that emerged from the ashes of the World Trade Center in New York, the real challenge to the Fukuyama thesis comes from the visible downgrading of the West's commitment to liberal democracy, ostensibly for the sake of homeland security. What we may be witnessing today is not history's end, but its retreat. The end of history thesis fails because the West's commitment to liberal democracy can no longer be viewed as linear and unconditional. In the West and elsewhere, homeland security now takes precedence over individual rights and civil liberties.

As the leader in the war on terror, the United States offers the most striking example of this shift. The American doctrine of homeland security envisages a pervasive surveillance of citizens unthinkable since the McCarthy era in the 1950s. A nationwide programme of turning ordinary citizens into informants and spies has been shelved, but other elements of homeland security continue to advance. The denial of prisoner of war rights to Afghan prisoners in Guantánamo Bay further attests to America's declining commitment to freedom.

US foreign policy reflects this shift as well. Attorney General John Ashcroft has openly praised internal security acts in Asia used to combat terror. American support for democratic transitions in the Third World, always selectively pursued, has eroded further.

With freedom in the United States under threat, America's Third World allies are less reticent about turning their own war on terror into a war against freedom. America has lost its moral high ground in the global human rights debate.

American support for the cause of self-determination and the human rights of ethnic minorities appears to have taken a backseat as Washington courts countries such as Russia (with its problems in Chechnya) as a strategic ally in the war against global terror.

Other nations, such as China and Burma, have seized the opportunity to link domestic ethnic separatism with the terrorist network.

Governments enjoying US support are using terrorism as an excuse to outmanoeuvre their political opponents. Even the differences between Europe and the US can be overstated. While the two disagree on strategic issues such as Iraq and Palestine, many nations in Europe too have embraced homeland security.

In the aftermath of September 11, 2001, states have curtailed market forces in their efforts to cut the financial lifelines of terrorist organizations. Transnational civil society networks, once seen as a catalyst of a more liberal world order, are under threat as many nongovernmental groups come under greater official surveillance for alleged links with terrorist groups.

The war on terror also gives ammunition to the critics of democracy and democratization as forces for peaceful change in international relations. As the case of the United States, India and Israel shows, democracies are no less vulnerable to terror, even though some argue that the spread of democracy could be a major step towards eradicating one of the root causes of terrorism.

Fukuyama is right in recognizing that the end of the history thesis was meant to apply to all of the West, including the United States. American unilateralism and US-Europe differences over Iraq and Palestine are therefore problematic. But what we are seeing today is not only a division of the West, but also its general retreat from Fukuyama's view of history.

22

Fear and Freedom in the Arab World

President Bush's November 2003 speech to the US Institute of Democracy was widely noted as one of the most important of his career. The speech made three points. First, it blamed Middle East's political and economic problems on a lack of freedom and openness. Second, it dismissed the view that Islam or Arab culture is inherently incompatible with democracy. Third, it conceded that "Sixty years of Western nations' excusing and accommodating the lack of freedom in the Middle East did nothing to make us safe".

The US victory over Iraq has created prospects for political change in the Middle East. Among the visions of a post-war Middle East offered by the Bush administration is the promotion of democracy in the Arab world. Regime change should not be confused with democratization. Democratization was not the original goal of the Bush administration when it made plans for war against Saddam. To quote Ari Fleischer, White House spokesman on April 11, 2003: "We have high confidence that they have weapons of mass destruction. This is what this war was and is about". If so, the war was not about democracy in the Arab world, but about punishing Iraq for stoking American fears about weapons of mass destruction. Regime change was a secondary goal. It was something needed to realize the goal of disarming Iraq.

The neo-conservatives in Washington who advocated regime change in Iraq are more concerned with the advancement of US interests and power than freedom and justice in the Arab world. Democratization is a convenient excuse to legitimize the raw assertion of US power and deter and punish competitors at the global and regional levels.

Second, there remains an important contradiction between US strategic interests and democratization, in what has been called the "democracy dilemma": how should the United States promote political liberalization without threatening core US interests in the Middle East? Many Arab countries which supported the war and have to be rewarded now are authoritarian. The victory over Saddam removes a major obstacle to regime change as a US political objective. This obstacle was the fact that many of the targets are US-friendly, offering cheap oil and access for US forces in the region. But with the US occupying Iraq, and the possibility that any new Iraqi regime will be obliging to US economic and strategic interests, there will be less inhibition on the part of the US to promote regime change. Yet, there is little prospect that the US will push for regime change in Kuwait or Saudi Arabia, either directly or indirectly, while counting on their support for military bases and oil supplies.

Hence, if the US is to promote democratization in these countries, it has to seek liberalization by the existing regimes, thus, is a much more difficult task. The contradiction between rewarding supporters and pushing them to change their ways will weigh heavily on American policymakers. This means that the targets of the democratization campaign will be divided into two camps: those who are pro-US will be treated lightly. Those who are anti-US, like Syria, will be targeted more aggressively, including with the use of force.

Democratization also risks bringing to power governments with anti-US values, especially among those with Islamist leadership. The Bush administration considers these worse than the status quo, since they would reject US influence in the Middle East. Past US administration have chosen authoritarianism over anti-US Islamist-oriented governments produced by democratic change. Short of direct US intervention in ensuring only pro-US regimes come into power, promoting democratization may be dangerous for US interests.

From a normative perspective, the spread of democratization is desirable. After the Cold War, Western policymakers and scholars had vigorously argued for democratization. Underlying this policy was a liberal doctrine of "democratic peace" which argues that democracies seldom go to war against each other and that a world of democracies will be more peaceful than a world of autocracies.

But the view has since been challenged, especially from academia. Critics of democratic peace have argued that the democratization process can lead to serious instability and war among states.

Moreover, whether democratization takes root in the region depends very much on how it is promoted. A key argument of scholars of democratic transitions has been that democracy cannot be imposed from outside. The challenge for the US, therefore, is to ensure that its agenda of democratization has the support of the Arab masses, especially the middle class. But herein lies an irony. The Arab middle class, which demands an end to authoritarian rule in their own societies, also opposed the US unilateralism and its support for Israel.

This brings us back to the Bush November 2003 speech, which claims to be a "forward strategy for freedom". But As Fareed Zakaria pointed out in his *Newsweek* column on November 17, 2003, "The "forward strategy" is never fleshed out, not even in a few lines, has no substantive elements to it and no programmes associated with it". More important, the speech did little to dampen fears that the goal of democratization may be pursued through force. While praising the Bush speech, ("as a lifelong advocate of democracy in the Arab world, I could not have written a better speech".) Saad Edin Ibrahim, a noted Egyptian dissident noted in the *Washington Post* on November 23, 2003: "there is a valid apprehension among Arab democrats about whether Washington is serious about supporting their efforts toward overdue democratic transformation. And if so, how will the United States go about it—with helpful encouragement or heavy-handed interference"?

There is little prospect that the goal of democratization through direct US pressure will apply to these regimes.

Amy Hawthorne of the Washington Institute for Near East Policy, in a provocative article "Do We Want Democracy In The Middle East?", points out that the Clinton administration found the costs of promoting democracy hard too high; and that "excessive" democracy in the Arab world was considered an impediment to securing top US strategic and economic objectives. The Clinton administration abandoned full-scale democratization and stressed "improved governance", "political participation", "pluralism", and "greater openness". The administration initiated democracy assistance initiatives to promote political reform and quality of governance to "to improve the climate for political liberalization in the region", according to a 1995 statement by then-Assistant Secretary of State for Near Eastern Affairs Robert H. Pelletreau.

An October 2002 Report entitled "Democratic Mirage in the Middle East", published by the Carnegie Endowment for International Peace, points out that the record of US promotion of democracy through intervention is not promising. The regime created by the US invasion of Haiti in 1994 did not lead to genuine democracy but political instability and renewed repression. Large-scale international aid produced stability and economic growth in Bosnia six years after the Dayton accords, but the political system remains fragile and might collapse if international forces leave. Panama offers a more positive example with some liberalization and pluralism after Noriega although it already had some experience with pluralism before Noriega. All these countries are small, hence manageable, unlike Iraq, with its 23 million inhabitants, which requires a much larger-scale effort. Here Afghanistan offers a dismal example. Early optimism after the Taliban period and the Bush administration's promises to lead the democratic reconstruction have not led to stability and certainty. The report points out that to promote democracy in Iraq, the US would have to become "engaged in nation building on a scale that would dwarf any other such effort since the reconstruction of Germany and Japan after World War II. And it would have to stay engaged not just years, but decades, given the depth of change required to make Iraq into a democracy".

Sceptics note that the Arab world lacks the necessary conditions for democratization, that it has no previous experience with democracy as did Central Europe, no sustained and prolonged economic growth producing dramatic changes in educational levels, nor the living standards that helped democratic change to evolve in Taiwan and South Korea. There has been no snowballing effect or positive neighbourhood effect creating regional pressure for democratization as in Latin America. Instead, we have rising fundamentalism, the worsening Arab-Israel conflict and the deepening negative perceptions of the US, all factors that would undermine the Bush administration's efforts to promote democracy in the Middle East.

Sources

Ari Fleisher, "U.S. Nearly Certain of Finding Iraqi Weapons", Agence France Presse, April 11, 2003.

Amy Hawthorne, "Do We Want Democracy in the Middle East?" at http://www.afsa.org/fsj/feb01/hawthorne01.cfm.

Dana Milbank and Mike Allen, "Bush Urges Commitment to Transform Mideast", *Washington Post*, November 7, 2003.

Fareed Zakaria, "Bush's Really Good Idea," *Newsweek*, November 17, 2003.

Washington Post, November 23, 2003.

Jennifer L. Windeerson, "Promoting Democratization Can Combat Terrorism," *Washington Quarterly*, Summer 2003.

Marina Ottawa, Thomas Carothers, Amy Hawthorne and Daniel Brumberg.

Democratic Mirage in the Middle East'.

Policy Brief 20 (Carnegie Endowment for International Peace, October 2002).

23

Fighting Terror in Southeast Asia

September 11 has led to a new counter-terrorism campaign in Southeast Asia with two main components. One is intra-regional cooperation among the ASEAN members. The second is their collaboration with Western powers, chiefly the US.

The impact of terrorism on regionalism in Southeast Asia is double-edged. It emerges as a common challenge that could galvanise regional cooperation. It could lead to new areas of cooperation, including information exchanges and measures to deal with money laundering and illegal migration. But such cooperation faces a number of constraints. The perception of the severity of the terrorist challenge varies even within ASEAN, making it difficult to devise common responses. Indonesia has been the key example of this, when Jakarta repeatedly refused to crack down on elements identified by its neighbours as leaders of Al-Qaeda-linked terrorist organizations. The Bali bombings of October 12, 2002 have since prompted Jakarta to toughen its stance on terrorism, including the passage of internal security measures, but the government risks domestic opposition to such measures, which will still constrain its response to terrorism.

Southeast Asia's response to terrorism has not brought Buddhist Burma and Thailand closer together. Nor has it prompted improved cooperation between Singapore and Malaysia or Singapore and Indonesia. The nation-state framework remains intact; the objective of regional cooperation is not so much to develop supra-national mechanisms as to beef up national capabilities. And there has been no compromise on ASEAN's non-interference doctrine. Cooperation undertaken by regional organizations focuses on intelligence and information exchanges, and regional capacity building rather than joint operational measures. Steps include cooperation amongst law agencies; exchange of information and intelligence on terrorist organizations, their movement and funding; as well as regional programmes for investigating, detecting, monitoring and reporting of terrorist acts. One of the more important initiatives undertaken in the region after September 11 was the signing of a trilateral agreement between Malaysia, Indonesia and the Philippines, to which Thailand and Cambodia have since joined. The Agreement provides for: anti-terrorism exercises as well as combined operations to hunt suspected terrorists, the setting up of hotlines and sharing of airline passenger lists, all of which are aimed at speeding intelligence exchanges between the three neighbours.

ASEAN and wider mechanisms of regional cooperation, such as the ASEAN Regional Forum (ARF) and the Asia Pacific Economic Cooperation (APEC) have also responded to the terrorist challenge. But caught in a moment of weakness caused by intramural bickering, the burdens of membership expansion and the lingering effects of the Asian economic crisis, Asian regional institutions have not been able to offer a strong response to the emerging transnational challenge, beyond the usual official statements and declarations. President Bush's attendance at the APEC Summit in Shanghai in 2001 served to underscore the importance it attaches to building a regional coalition against terror. But beyond this symbolic move, the focus of America's war on terror continues to be in South Asia and the Middle East. The ARF in July 2002 called for freezing terrorist assets, as well as greater international cooperation on the exchange of information and outreach, and compliance and reporting. It formed an Inter-Sessional Group (ISG) on counter-Terrorism and Translational Crime (co-chaired by Malaysia and the US). The UN remains the key framework. The 5 November 2001 ASEAN Declaration urged members towards ratification of all anti-terrorist conventions, including the International Convention for the Suppression of the Financing of Terrorism. It urged compliance with UN instruments and resolutions. Bilateral or subregional (sub-ASEAN) frameworks have been preferred over purely multilateral ones.

But there remain important obstacles to closer regional cooperation, obstacles which have to do with national priorities, domestic politics, interstate discord, differing national capacities and dependence on outside powers. This brings us to the second major component of counter-terrorism in Southeast Asia: collaboration with the US and participation in the US-led war on terror.

In Southeast Asia, the post-Cold War era began with plenty of uncertainty about the US military presence in the region, which many regional governments have long regarded as a crucial stabilising factor.

By the late-1990s, this concern had been substantially alleviated, thanks to repeated US assurances to that effect, and the "revitalization" of the US-Japan alliance under the Nye Initiative. However, Southeast Asia remained a relatively marginal spot in US strategic priorities, which continued to focus on Europe, the Middle East and Northeast Asia.

In the post-post Cold War era that emerged from the ashes of the World Trade Center, Southeast Asian status in US strategic policy has changed dramatically. It's now regarded as a Second Front in the war against terrorism, commanding a great deal of US attention and resources. And Southeast Asian worries about US withdrawal have given way to mounting concerns about US unilateralism.

The US approach to terrorism is overwhelmingly strategic, military assistance, economic aid and security agreements have not been backed by efforts to address what is perceived in Southeast Asia as a fundamental root cause of contemporary Islamic radicalism", namely, the issue of Palestine.

The US dramatically enhanced its strategic role in the region, especially in the Philippines, where it conducted joint "exercises" with local troops against the Abu Sayyaf group. For the Philippines, increased American presence and strategic links with the US not only helps its resource-starved military to gain access to vital US equipment, it also mitigates Manila's immediate and long-term concerns about the rise of Chinese power. A new logistics agreement with the US negotiated in the context of the war on terror could also be a strategic asset to Manila in their efforts to counter future Chinese encroachments in the disputed territories in the South China Sea.

As the world's largest Muslim nation, Jakarta is an attractive ally for the US in its eagerness to correct the perception of the war against terror as a war against Islam. This was evident during Megawati's visit to the White House (she being the first leader of a Muslim majority nation to do so in the aftermath of September 11). George W. Bush received her warmly and offered increased economic aid. Malaysian Prime Minister Mohamad, known for his strong criticism of US hegemony, visited Washington and also won recognition for Malaysia as a modern Muslim state that has taken a firm stand against radical Islam. For Malaysia, the war on terror presented an opportunity to gain US recognition for its role in regional affairs. Following September 11, however, US-Malaysian ties have improved considerably. Malaysia has sought and earned American sympathy and support as well as praise as the model of a progressive and moderate Muslim nation. The US and Malaysia have signed a bilateral agreement on information-sharing and other forms of cooperation against terrorism. Even more striking is the American Attorney-General's endorsement of Malaysia's Internal Security Act, which is viewed now by the US as less as an threat to civil liberties and more as a vital instrument to fight terror.

The US also signed an agreement with ASEAN providing for cooperation on a number of issues, including intelligence-sharing. US Singapore-relations, already cemented by agreements to support US military deployments out of Singapore facilities, have been furthered strengthened. Even Burma, which sees terrorism as a common menace, has pledged to "stand side by side" with the US in fighting terrorism.

Indonesia's domestic politics remain important in constraining US security cooperation with that country. Upon returning home from her visit to Washington, the Indonesian president found her domestic situation sufficiently difficult so as to distance herself from the US attack on the Taliban. Jakarta brushed aside American (and Singaporean) accusations of turning itself into a safe haven for Al-Qaeda elements. Even in the wake of the horrific Bali attacks, Jakarta faces domestic pressure to take action against the suspected terrorist elements. While it has passed new internal security regulations, the arrest of JI's spiritual leader Abu Bakar Bashir was criticized even by some moderate political leaders as a capitulation to US demands.

The key determinants of the war on terror in Southeast Asia are domestic politics, conventional national interest calculations and common fear. The latter, fear, has produced some degree of regional cooperation, but not to the degree that might offset the perception of Asian regional institutions as being weak and process-oriented notwithstanding their professed commitment to multilateralism. The perception of the sources or root causes of terrorism among Southeast Asian countries has differed in important ways from that of the Bush administration. But societal anti-Americanism has not prevented governments from undertaking close cooperation with the US. Political rhetoric aside, pragmatism has prevailed over principle in Southeast Asia's war against terror.

24

Asia Between America and Europe

In a much-debated article, entitled "Power and Weakness" appearing in the American journal *Policy Review* (June–July 2002), Robert Kagan presents a powerful contrast between American and European attitudes towards power and international relations. He makes two important points. First, Americans and Europeans (allowing for oversimplification of both categories) live in very different worlds and represent two increasingly divergent worldviews and strategic cultures. The Europeans are "Kantians" who have entered "a post-historical paradise of peace and relative prosperity". They favour peaceful solutions to international problems through diplomacy, persuasion and negotiation. The Americans live and believe in a "Hobbesian" world in which international rules are deemed inefficient and unreliable and where security and order is seen to depend on the "possession and use of military might".

Kagan explains this divergence between America and Europe chiefly in terms of a widening gap of physical power. America emerged from the Cold War as the world's sole superpower. Left unchecked by countervailing Soviet power and helped by a booming economy, America could keep and reorient its powerful military to engage in increasing number of overseas military interventions. Meanwhile, Europe reduced its defence expenditures and moved increasingly on the path of regional accommodation and integration. Its relative power declined steadily, notwithstanding earlier predictions about a united Europe emerging as a superpower in its own right.

Where does Asia fit in this growing Euro-American divergence? Although limited to a broad-brush comparison of American and European strategic conditions and predicaments, Kagan's perspective allows us to place Asia in a larger global strategic context.

The world in which Asians live and the worldview to which most Asian leaders subscribe appear to be more Hobbesian than Kantian. Unlike Europe, Asia remains rife with conflicts. It lags far behind Europe's level of regional integration and its commitment to liberal democracy. Moreover, while relative lack of power vis-à-vis the US is common to both Europe and Asia, this has produced dissimilar responses. Kagan holds that Europe's lack of power has led it increasingly on the path of multilateralism. In the case of Asia, it has led to strategic dependence on larger players, particularly the United States. While military alliances are in decline in Europe, they remain robust in Asia.

Yet, Asians are not, and cannot be, Hobbesian in the sense that America is. Unlike the US, Asia lacks the means to pursue national objectives unilaterally through force. Asia is too conscious of its vulnerabilities and weaknesses to share America's "culture of death", i.e., its tendency to view the world in "good versus evil" terms, its "warlike temperament", and its penchant for "coercion" and "unilateralism" over diplomacy and cooperation to attain national objectives. Indeed, both Europeans and Asians share a common fear of these aspects of US hegemony. Kagan asserts that compared to Americans, Europeans are "more tolerant of failure, more patient when solutions don't come quickly". They eschew "finality" in international affairs, prefer "negotiation, diplomacy, and persuasion", and emphasize "process over result". Many of these observations are true of Asians as well.

Moreover, differences between the trajectories of order in Europe and Asia should not be overstated. Asia may never become, or aspire to become, a Kantian paradise. But conditions for order based on Kantian formulations have emerged. In the early Cold War period, Asia's regional order rested on three pillars: (1) inward-looking, nationalist and state-led economic development strategies; (2) authoritarian rule with the significant exceptions of India and Japan; and (3) bilateral alliances with major powers, especially the US. Today, these have given way to shared economic liberalism (export-led growth, free trade and growing regional economic interdependence), democratic transitions in many countries, and the emergence of regional institutions. The fact is that Asia today is much more interdependent, democratic and institutionalized than at the beginning of the post-World War II period.

Hence, absolute categories such as Hobbesian or Kantian do not do an adequate job of explaining Asia's complex and fluid security predicament. Moreover, the power gap emphasized by Kagan in explaining the Euro-American divergence is not the sole or the most important determinant of Asia's attitude towards international relations. Culture, norms and identity also matter. Despite growing divergence, there is far greater convergence of identity between Europeans and Americans than between Asians on the one hand and the Europeans and the Americans on the other. In addition, Asia itself is culturally far less homogenous within itself than Europe or America. These intra-Asian differences make it more difficult to speak of a single "Asian" attitude towards international relations. Just as there is no single Asian approach to peace, there can also be no single Asian condition of anarchy or disorder. Moments and pockets of stability will co-exist with areas of chaos and disorder.

While Europe's commitment to multilateralism and rule of law in international affairs is born out of a determination to transcend the sovereignty-bound nation-state system, Asia's interest in multilateralism is born primarily out of a desire to preserve the existing rules of international relations, especially those related to sovereignty. Europeans increasingly live in a post-sovereign world, believing it to be more efficient and morally desirable; Asians remain firmly beholden to sovereignty, taking it as the fundamental basis of their stability and identity. Asians, like Europeans, oppose American unilateralism, as evident in recent debates about Iraq. But Asians have done so less out of moral compulsions than a fear of legitimizing great power intervention in their internal affairs. Thus, while Europe pursues a principled multilateralism and American an instrumental one (selective and serving American national interests and need), Asian multilateralism is conditioned by essentially pragmatic concerns geared towards state and regime survival.

Epilogue: "Europe's foreign policy pipe dream is shattered," so runs the headline of an article by William Safire in the *International Herald Tribune* on February 11, 2003.

The split started over a letter written by the leaders of eight European countries (Britain, Italy, Spain, Portugal, Poland, Hungary, Denmark and the Czech Republic) backing the American stand on Iraq. What is more, it dashed the view that France and Germany, as the "core" of Europe, could dictate the foreign policy of Europe.

It might be argued that France and Germany are playing domestic politics. But what this suggests is that a shared liberal democratic political system and beliefs do not guarantee unity over key foreign policy issues. Europe is more Kantian than Asian, but some parts of Europe are less Kantian than others.

The split in Europe has an important message for Asia. Asian regionalism is in some disarray since the 1997 economic crisis. The once cohesive ASEAN is no longer so. Asian states have taken no common stand over Iraq. Asian regional institutions are essentially preoccupied with local security issues. Asian states have not adopted a common attitude towards terrorism. They maintain different attitudes towards US unilateralism. Their security ties with the US vary from country to country.

Should this be seen as the end of Asian regionalism? Compared to Asian regional groups, NATO and the EU are considered to be strong regional institutions. EU aspiring to a common security and defence policy. But the public display of disunity over what might be a defining issue of the post-September 11 era does not bode well for European regionalism. National interest still rules over regional integration and supranationalism.

If the EU after such a long evolution could not agree on Iraq, why should one expect Asia with its more recent history of regionalism to act united?

25

Asia's Response to the Bush Doctrine

A major development affecting US-Asian relations after September 11, 2001 is the new American strategic doctrine of "pre-emptive" strikes. Some Asian critics, especially Malaysia's Prime Minister Mahathir, have viewed the Bush Doctrine as a dangerous approach. The doctrine, its critics argue, gives Washington a blank cheque to strike any regime deemed unfriendly to the US, and which can be linked to terrorism or some other pretext. The doctrine would lead to hasty military action without exhausting all possible diplomatic means. Also important is its flouting of the sovereignty principle. Furthermore, critics see the doctrine as a clear example of the US turn towards unilateralism, giving America the right to use force without authorization from the UN Security Council. It is seen against the backdrop of a long and growing list of US actions against multilateral institutions, including the International Criminal Court, the Kyoto Protocol, and the *Anti-Ballistic Missile Treaty (ABM)*. Moreover, critics see the doctrine as a pretext for the US to pursue its other strategic and economic interests through military force. For example, an occupation of Iraq, ostensibly to eliminate weapons of mass destruction and human rights abuses, will also put under American control one of the world's largest proven reserves of oil.

While the US itself has not made any Southeast Asian state a target of pre-emption, its closest ally, Australia, which under the Howard government has proclaimed itself as a "deputy sheriff" to the US, has not been so reticent. Australia has announced its own pre-emptive strategy, the "Howard corollary". Howard's pro-US stance meant that it was seen to some extent as an extension of the Bush Doctrine to Southeast Asia. The US helped to further this perception by openly endorsing the Australian Prime Minister's stance.

The US strike on Iraq brought out some of the reservations held by Southeast Asian states regarding the Bush Doctrine in particular and the US war on terror in general. There were major public demonstrations against the war in Malaysia and Indonesia.

While Singapore openly backed the war, many other Southeast Asian countries remain unconvinced of the rationale for a US strike on Iraq. The Bush administration's claim that war was necessary to rid the world of a regime that threatened US and global security by quietly but surely building up an arsenal of deadly weapons of mass destruction, was viewed with widespread skepticism in the region.

It would have been politically easier for Southeast Asian countries to support the US had Washington secured the Security Council's formal authorization for a strike on Iraq after the submission of the report of the UN inspectors. In the absence of this, the strike on Iraq heightened perceptions in Southeast Asia of US unilateralism and arrogance. Southeast Asian governments faced the possibility of a popular Muslim backlash if they were to support the war against Iraq. Moreover, given that no credible evidence linking the Saddam Hussein regime with Al-Qaeda was forthcoming from the US, Southeast Asian countries viewed the Iraqi issue as a huge distraction from the war on terrorism, which for them is a much more urgent and important challenge. When North Korea disclosed its secret nuclear weapons programme, Southeast Asian critics of the war against Iraq, especially Malaysian leaders, accused the US of double standards. North Korea's nuclear programme is more advanced than Iraq's. Since the main reason for going to war against Saddam is its programme of weapons of mass destruction, critics of the Bush Doctrine asked whether the same logic should not apply to North Korea.

As the controversy over the Howard statement died down, the US attack on Iraq became the other major occasion for debate and dissent over the Bush Doctrine in Asia.

India became one of the first Asian countries to speak the language of pre-emption. In early April 2003, soon after the US went to war in Iraq, India's Foreign Minister Yashwant Sinha told parliament that India had "a much better case to go for pre-emptive action against Pakistan than the US has in Iraq". In his view, Pakistan's nuclear capability and its support for the Kashmir groups make it a "fitter case" for intervention than Iraq. Moreover, Pakistan fulfilled the third criterion laid down by the Bush doctrine on pre-emption: being ruled by an authoritarian regime state. Ignoring US objections to this viewpoint, Defence Minister George Fernandes supported Sinha, although he somewhat qualified his support by making a distinction between intention and reality: "No, we are not talking about any intention here. There is no intention as such, but whatever he has said is correct".

Pakistan, which opposed the Bush Doctrine, reacted to the Indian statement strongly. Prime Minister Zafarullah Khan Jamali and Foreign Minister Khurshid Mahmood Kasuri called Sinha's talk of pre-emptive operations "ridiculous". In a statement, the Pakistani foreign minister said: "India should not harbour any illusions of launching pre-emptive strikes against Pakistan, as it would constitute a major miscalculation on its part". "We know how to defend ourselves", Jamali said at a Cabinet meeting.

The US has argued that while pre-emptive attacks were permissible in the case of Iraq, the same logic does not hold for India, which is fighting Pakistan-sponsored terrorism, or for China, which wants to reunify with Taiwan. As White House Press Secretary Ari Fleischer puts it, "What is different is the unique history of Iraq. Different policies work in different parts of the world, and different doctrines work at different times and in different regions because of local circumstances". This was a much more qualified version of the Bush Doctrine than what its original formulation had implied. China too rejected India's right of pre-emption. Its Foreign Ministry spokesman Liu Jianchao stated: "China has always held that conflicts or disputes between states should be solved peacefully through dialogue instead of resorting to force or the threat of use of force". "India and Pakistan are countries of importance in South Asia and have great responsibility in maintaining peace and stability in the region".

Subsequently, India toned down its stance on pre-emption. Kanwal Sibal, India's foreign secretary said that comparisons between Pakistan and Iraq were rhetorical in nature and were not intended as "advance indication for any kind of imminent action" against Pakistan. Fernandes described the talk about pre-emption as a "casual statement and not any policy decision of the government or a considered view of some section".

China has taken a firm stance against the Bush Doctrine. According to Chinese Foreign Ministry Spokesman Liu Jianchao, while China is a staunch supporter of the fight against all forms of terrorism, it was also of the opinion that strikes must be based on "conclusive evidence, clear-cut targets and in accordance with the Charter of the United Nations and international codes of conduct". Some analysts have speculated whether the US strike on Iraq might lead China to consider developing its own pre-emptive strategy to deal with its "rogue" province, Taiwan. According to one view, China may be "calculating how successful use of pre-emption by the US in Iraq can be applied to Taiwan...any action that moves Taiwan further from China or closer to de jure independence—for example increasing US arms sales or including Taiwan in a regional missile defence system—will trigger a strong reaction from Beijing. Having set the precedent of pre-emption where vital national interests are at stake, the US can expect China to follow suit.

Given North Korea's status as a charter member of the "Axis of Evil", it is only natural that it would be at the centre of questions about "after Iraq: what"? South Korea's new president Roh Moo-Hyun, who has a declaratory commitment to his predecessors' policy of closer engagement with North Korea has been especially nervous about the extension of the Bush Doctrine to the Korean Peninsula. In his words: "I would like to discuss with President Bush that the circumstances on the Korean Peninsula may not be appropriate for applying this principle [of pre-emption] from the very beginning. The mere thought of a military conflict with North Korea is a calamity for us". As Roh sees it, the answer to the inter-Korean situation is not pre-emption but dialogue.

Whether North Korea is a ripe target for pre-emption is a matter of some debate. "What the cases of North Korea and Iraq show is that if the threat is genuinely serious, the pre-emption doctrine is not pursued", said Zbigniew Brzezinski, who was national security adviser to President Jimmy Carter. "If the threat is not immediate but, as the president said, grave and gathering, then you rely on pre-emption. It is less risky and more satisfying to beat up someone who is less threatening than more threatening". Another sceptic, Philip Bowring, a former editor of the *Far Eastern Economic Review*, points out that while "The pre-war shift of US policy from deterrence to pre-emption had aroused plenty of concern in the region, but only in South Korea did discussion of its consequences get beyond the academic. On North Korea, the United States seems to have little option but dialogue other than a pre-emptive strike, the thought of which horrifies all of East Asia".

Other critics have based their doubts about the Bush Doctrine on the grounds that the situation in North Korea may be too late for pre-emption. On the other side are those who believe that pre-emption in the Korean Peninsula is quite doable, especially with some adjustments to the US force deployments in South Korea. According to arch-conservative *New York Times* columnist William Safire, "While defeating Saddam Hussein, the United States let it be known that it was prepared to pull its 37,000 tripwire troops out of harm's way along the Demilitarised Zone, opening the possibility of an air assault on plutonium production". Safire and others argued that the Iraqi example prompted North Korea to take a more moderate posture: a shift from brinkmanship to diplomacy. The subsequent hints from the US suggesting a withdrawal from the DMZ area to a more rear position lends some credence to this perspective.

While the Bush team's aim to make the US safe from weapons of mass destruction and international terrorists will remain imperative, the goal of regime change will face several reality checks. For example, regime change in North Korea through military intervention may not be worth the risk or has to be attempted differently than that in Iraq. One has to be careful about generalizing from the Iraq episode about how the US will respond to other, apparently similar challenges. Likewise, for political and economic reasons, the US will not reject international cooperation in every instance, although the appeal of the UN to a serving US president is clearly at its lowest point in memory.

Japan's own turn to pre-emption has been most clearly led by Defence Minister Shigeru Ishiba. Ishiba believes that a pre-emptive strike would be a logical response to an impending North Korea missile attack. "It is too late if [a missile] flies towards Japan. Our nation will use military force as a self-defence measure if [North Korea] starts to resort to arms against Japan". Ishiba further added that if necessary, Japanese pre-emption could be independent of the US, since there was no such thing as "a free ride in the post-Cold War era". He also downplayed possible constitutional barriers: "Japan's constitution doesn't intend that we just wait and be attacked. This is not just what I think. It should be decided according to popular opinion and from listening to the Japanese people". In comments clearly directed at North Korea, Japanese Prime Minister Junichiro Koizumi told Parliament that if the Japanese government believed that a foreign country had a clear intention or plan to invade Japan "we could not just let the Japanese people be harmed by doing nothing". Although Koizumi has said that Japan will not alter its "exclusively defensive defence", Ishiba has indicated that, when the US launches a pre-emptive attack in the Pacific like that in the Iraq war, "it is by no means impossible" that Japan would invoke its "emergencies legislation" to help the US military. In this sense, the Bush Doctrine has become the rationale and spur for Japan's own pre-emptive strategy.

Given the range of responses to the Bush Doctrine in Asia, it is important to ask: has there been any impact of Asian criticisms of the Bush Doctrine on the administration's policy? At the second annual Shangri-la Dialogue held in Singapore during May 31–June 1, 2003, Deputy Secretary of Defense Wolfowitz made a surprising statement that "the pre-emptive part of the NSS (National Security Strategy) is a bit overstated." He also took care to describe the action in Iraq as "preventive" action, rather than "pre-emptive". Moreover, Wolfowtiz insisted that pre-emption would be discriminating between cases, although it is now introduced to the vocabulary and remains firmly within the "menu of choice".

To sum up, in considering the determinants of Asian governments' responses to the Bush Doctrine, three appear especially noteworthy. First, domestic considerations have played an important role in several states. Such concerns were especially salient in the case of the Roh administration in South Korea, which had come into power on a platform that stressed the engagement of North Korea and a politically acceptable redeployment of US forces in South Korea. In Southeast Asia, governments in the Islamic majority states, especially Malaysia and Indonesia, were worried that public endorsement of the Bush Doctrine would invite popular backlash. While these states were willing partners of the US in the war against terrorism, they wished to keep security collaboration with the US as low key and covert as possible. Even Thailand, a member of America's system of bilateral alliances, stayed away from the coalition of the willing against Iraq. In contrast, the Howard government in Australia played to a domestic audience in a climate of heightened nationalism generated by the Bali bombings in advancing its own idea of pre-emption.

A second factor shaping Asian attitudes towards the Bush Doctrine is normative. The extent to which the doctrine presaged military action to bring about regime change it conflicted with the widespread appeal of, sovereignty and the non-interference norms in Asia.

Third, Asian governments have been genuinely concerned about the Bush administration's scant regard for multilateralism, especially at the global level. While many Asian states support, or can at least live with, the US primary, they also regard the UN system of vital importance to regimal and international security order. Lee Kuan Yew, Singapore's Senior Minister and an otherwise staunch ally of the US, warned the Bush administration of the consequences of unilateralism in a *Straits Times* article that appeared on May 31, 2003: "Throughout history, every force has generated a counter-force. For the present, Russia, China and many countries in the European Union want to maintain good or friendly relations with the US. There is reason to hope that tending to these relations can prolong US pre-eminence. Not to do so may persuade more nations that the way to restraint American unilateralism is to join a group of all those opposed to it".

Sources

"China joins in criticism of Howard's pre-emptive strike policy", *Channel News Asia*, December 4, 2002.

"China opposes Indian threat of pre-emptive strikes", *Pakistan Newswire*, April 8, 2003.

"Foreign ministry spokesman on Australia's pre-emptive strike proposal", in *Xinhua General News Service*, section: domestic news political, December 3, 2002.

"Indian DM downplays remarks on pre-emptive strikes on Pakistan", *Xinhua News Agencies*, April 12, 2003.

"Indian minister ignores U.S remarks, says Pakistan fit for pre-emptive strike", in BBC monitoring south-Asia-political supplied by *BBC Worldwide Monitoring*, April 11, 2003.

"India's threat of preemption stirs alarm", *Inter Press Service*, April 8, 2003.

"Japan debates a first-strike defense", *The Age* (Melbourne), May 22, 2003.

"Japan studied strike against North Korea to prevent missile attack: report", the *Times* (London), May 22, 2003.

"Japan strike threat to Korea", *Sydney Morning Herald*, February 15, 2003.

"Japan threatens force against North Korea", BBC News, February 14, 2003.

"Japan wants pre-emptive policy", *Australian Financial Review*, May 22, 2003.

"Preemption is dangerous", *Global News Wire*, April 10, 2003.

Liu Jianchao, "China-India", in 'the press trust of India', section: Nationwide International News, 8 April 2003.

"Pakistan warns India of grave consequences of pre-emptive strikes", *Xinhua News Agency*, April 3, 2003.

Personal notes of the Shangri-la dialogue, Singapore, May 31–June 1, 2003.

Lee Kuan Yew, *Straits Times*, May 31, 2003.

Phillip Bowring, "Asia is waiting to see how America handles victory", *International Herald Tribune*, April 22, 2003.

"Preemption not permissible for India against Pak: white house", *Indian Express*, May 23, 2003.

Rob Radtke, "Iraq effect on U.S role in Asia", *Christian Science Monitor*, May 8, 2003, online at www.csmonitor.com/2003/0508/p11s02-coop.html.

Robert A. Levine, "Preemption didn't win", *International Herald Tribune*, April 22, 2003.

"U.S keeps preemption doctrine 'open'; rebuffs Roh's call to exempt North Korea", *Washington Times*, May 13, 2003.

William Safire, "Preemption Proves Itself", *International Herald Tribune*, April 15, 2003.

26

Terror and the Asian Balance of Power

Among the more fundamental outcomes produced by the September 11, 2001 attacks on the United States and its subsequent global war on terror is the uncertain fate of the Asian balance of power system. Conventional strategic thinking (both in Asia and the West) has long credited Asia's balance of power system with the maintenance of the region's peace and prosperity.

During the Cold War, the Asian balance of power was essentially a subset of the global balance of terror between the two superpowers, rather than reflective of a rough parity in their conventional military strength. It masked a fundamental asymmetry of power between the US and its main rivals, namely the Soviet Union and China. Under the façade of academic claims about the existence of a balance of power, the US actually maintained an unprecedented and largely unchallenged hegemony on the ground. While this global balance of terror did prevent major war between the US and the Soviet Union, it was also a remarkably limited instrument. It did not prevent large-scale domestic instability, such as Indonesia in 1965 and in Cambodia during the Khmer Rouge regime. Nor did it necessarily ensure stability in intra-regional relationships, such as that between China and its neighbours, or in subregional relationships, such as between Vietnam and ASEAN. Moreover, it created a questionable sense of complacency that reduced the urgency of building a more comprehensive and durable basis for regional order.

In the early 1990s, the proponents of the US-led balance of power system had reason to worry when the US pulled its bases out of the Philippines and an embryonic multilateral cooperative security arrangement began to emerge in the region. The prospects for a US strategic retrenchment in the region seemed possible, if not imminent.

The terrorist attacks on the US on September 11, 2001 removed that possibility. It prompted a rethink of the relative strategic importance of regional theatres for US grand strategy. While the importance of the Middle East as part of America's sphere of vital interests is expectedly confirmed, South Asia now would have a higher profile in US grand strategy than was the case for some time. Moreover, American strategic engagement in Southeast Asia has been strengthened. Apart from being regarded as the second front in the war against terrorism, Southeast Asia became important to the US for overflight and access rights for its military deployments to the Gulf. During the war against the Taliban in 2001, the US found it easier to secure overflight rights through Southeast Asia than through Europe. Southeast Asian worries about US withdrawal have now given way to mounting concerns about US unilateralism.

The extent of US engagement in Southeast Asia should not be overstated. Critics note that while the United States has clearly recognized Southeast Asia's potential to be a safe haven from Al-Qaeda fugitives and homegrown terrorists, its strategic priorities remain firmly focused elsewhere, namely the Middle East, South and Central Asia and Northeast Asia. The offer of economic assistance to Indonesia, an information-sharing agreement with Malaysia and the conduct of joint "training" operations with the Philippines, do not make for full-scale strategic engagement. While Southeast Asia enjoys a higher profile in US strategy, this is still not comparable to the US engagement with India and Pakistan or in Central Asia.

While the US response to the threat of terrorism affects the region as a whole, its most visible impact is felt in the maritime domain of Southeast Asia, where the dangers seems most apparent. This domain comprises Malaysia, the Philippines, Singapore and Indonesia. Among ASEAN countries, Singapore is most appreciative of the US' response to the threat of transnational terrorism in Southeast Asia as a catalyst for a more favourable regional balance of power. This accords with Singapore's traditional preference for US military predominance in the region as the regional balancer. Singapore has maintained significant military links with the US, including serving as a major logistics hub for US naval forces operating in the region (this relationship, of course, predates September 11), and making facilities available for US operations against Iraq.

September 11 affected the security postures and relationships among the major powers. Overall, it confirmed US preponderance. There is little prospect for an alternative Asian coalition challenging US predominance. September 11 did produce a nominal improvement in great power relations. But the most visible improvement was between the US and other major players, particularly China, India and Russia. The warmth in US-Russian relations sparked by Putin's sympathy and support for the US was not dampened by Russian troops' dash to Afghanistan soon after its liberation from the Taliban. The terrorist attacks diverted attention from Sino-US tensions, eased by China's support, albeit qualified, for the US anti-terrorist campaign. And US-India relations have become probably the warmest than anytime in history.

On the other hand, Beijing could not have been happy with the haste with which the Japanese government pushed through legislation to enable its navy (in a supporting role) to enter the waters of the Indian Ocean for the first time since World War II in war time. Sino-Indian tensions continue over Beijing's support for the Pakistani military.

Hence, the US-led balance of power structure remains alive and well in Asia. But can it bring about security in Asia? Before September 11, the conventional strategic wisdom in and about Asia portrayed the rise of China (albeit vastly exaggerated by China's critics and admirers alike) as the principal challenge to regional security. September 11, 2001 demonstrated that the threat to peace in Asia today comes not from a rival rising power, as once feared by many regional governments, but from an invisible and insidious network of terror that feeds upon the region's cultural faultlines, weak governance structures, economic disparities and lack of democratic space.

The efficacy of a US-led security structure can be undermined as much by rising rivals as by the declining international legitimacy of the leading power responsible for its maintenance. As the relative hard power of the US reaches its zenith, in Asia the US has shown a marked aversion to the exercise of soft power, especially multilateralism, with a consequent erosion of its legitimacy as a world leader. The war of terror conducted largely through military means without regard for its root causes such as economic disparities (as opposed to poverty), political grievances of the people, and injustices suffered by the Palestinians, has further contributed to the erosion of the legitimacy of American power. Hence, the idea of "benign hegemony" that underpinned regional security in Asia may be coming to grief.

America's Asian alliances are under increasing pressure from America's rising hegemony. Western strategic analysts have often stressed the superiority of Europe's NATO-led multilateral alliance structure over Asia's hubs-and-spoke system. But under conditions of extreme hegemony as prevails today, and in the absence of a clearly visible and identifiable threat, Asia's bilateral alliance structure may prove easier to maintain and manipulate than Europe's multilateral structure, as the US is finding out in relation to NATO. Yet the efficacy of alliances is also undermined by growing power asymmetries. As the US military grows more technologically sophisticated, inter-operability in Asia will be undermined as America's Asian allies increasingly fall behind the leader.

The growing anti-Americanism in Asia on the mass politics level also increases the political costs for regimes who have thrown their lot behind the US in the war against terror. This comes at a time when many regimes in Asia face a democratic deficit, aggravated by the regional economic downturn, and who are now more liable to be portrayed by their people as being unduly subservient to the US.

There continue to be important divergences in the strategic perceptions and priorities between the US and its closest regional partners. The increased level of US military presence does not mean the US has secured permanent military bases. Even in the Philippines, where the US was kicked out in the early 1990s, negotiations for long-term access have been stymied by Philippine domestic sensitivities, as well as US reluctance to link its presence their with Manila's dispute with China over the Spratlys.

In Asia, regional multilateral groups such as ASEAN have contributed to the construction and development of a security order by careful adjustments in their strategic policy and by seeking to engage bigger powers such as China and the United States into a shared normative framework. Yet, Asia's multilateral institutions are being ignored by the US and its like-minded allies. The region is thus deprived of an opportunity to construct and maintain a wider basis for regional security relations, which can address and compensate for the deficiencies of a power-balancing system.

Many Asian elites have grown accustomed to viewing America's forward military presence and its alliances as a regional public good that underpins Asia's economic growth and regional stability. If this view is correct, shouldn't they be reassured by American growing power today? But the aftermath of September 11 suggests the potential for the opposite outcome. An American-led balance of power remains an essential ingredient for peace in Asia. But its legitimacy and hence efficacy cannot be taken for granted.

27

India From Nehru to Curzon

A new book by C. Raja Mohan meticulously documents how September 11 helped move India's foreign policy away from Nehruvian "idealism" to a new realism rooted in what the Foreign Minister of the time, Jaswant Singh, would wistfully describe as neo-Curzonian geopolitics. Entitled *Crossing the Rubicon*, the book describes the BJP's (the Bharatiya Janata Party) shift towards a foreign policy which places India's security interests at the heart of an Asian geopolitical order.

In this perspective, Curzon is cast as one of the greatest Indian "nationalists" because of his role in positioning India as the centre of gravity in the British empire and securing India's territorial interests. As Raja Mohan puts it, Curzon "dreamt of a powerful role for India in its surrounding regions" and "emphasised India's centrality in the Indian Ocean littoral". He quotes Curzon's 1909 essay, *The Place of India in the Empire*, which argued, among other things, that India was the:

> greatest power in the Asiatic Continent, and therefore, in the world ... The Central position of India, its magnificent resources, its teeming multitude of men, its great trading harbours, its reserve of military strength, supplying an army always in a high state of efficiency and capable of being hurled at a moment's notice upon any point either of Asia and Africa—all these are assets of precious value.

Two things prevented India from realizing this vision: the partition of India by the departing British and Nehru's alleged idealism (which to this author, is a false impression; Nehru was a realist, a different kind than Curzon or the BJP, but a realist nonetheless). Jaswant Singh is said to be "sharply critical of the failure of Jawaharlal Nehru in creating a strategic culture suited to its geographic circumstances", according to Raja Mohan.

The new turn in Indian foreign policy predated September 11 and involved the virtual abandonment of non-alignment in favour of a tight security relationship with the US. Its new foreign policy came to be marked by a growing suspicion of multilateralism, especially the Clinton era approach which put India at the receiving end of UN-backed condemnation and anti-proliferation sanctions.

Thanks to the war on terror, India no longer has much to fear from the US on this front. The post-September 11 milieu allowed India to decisively break out of the isolation caused by its nuclear tests. Many geopolitical pundits predicted significant gains for New Delhi's global and regional influence in a way Curzon might have liked. New Delhi was able to reframe the Kashmir issue as a terrorist threat, rather than a freedom struggle issue. By playing to American concerns against terrorism, India has been able to score diplomatic points vis-à-vis Pakistan points, that spotlighting Pakistan's support for terrorism and its involvement in the transfer of weapons of mass destruction technology. In the post-Taliban era, Delhi gained influence in Afghanistan at the expense of Pakistan, the creator of Taliban. Delhi also consolidated its security ties with Washington. Some pundits foresaw New Delhi gaining influence in its neighbourhood at China's expense. Aided by the US, Pakistan would become less dependent on China. India's strategic position vis-à-vis China should be strengthened by the growing US military presence in Central Asia, where China had painstakingly built up its own anti-terror alliance and was in the process of securing its own long-term access to the region's oil.

But such zero-sum geopolitical thinking is misplaced. To be sure, India now has more influence in Afghanistan in the post-Taliban era. Cooperation against terrorism has extended India's reach into Southeast Asia, where it has conducted joint patrolling of the strategic Straits of Malacca with US forces to guard against threats to shipping. But India's gains have not come at the expense of China, at least in Southeast Asia. More importantly, India's gains have come firmly within the framework of Washington's strategic framework in the region, over which New Delhi has little real influence.

South Asia has become a focal point of the US-led global anti-terror campaign. The US has secured military access rights not only in Central Asia but has also been offered and used military facilities in both Pakistan and India. In this process, the role of Pakistan has been rather substantial, with Pakistani forces coordinating and collaborating in US anti-terror operations. The US has used its presence to extend its influence into other parts of the region—supporting Kathmandu's fight against the Maoists, coaxing and prodding the LTTE in Sri Lanka to move ahead with the Norwegian-brokered peace process and nudging and encouraging the government of Bangladesh to monitor and rein in the extremist groups especially as the groups have fallen prey to international Islamic extremist groups. The net outcome has been an unprecedented level of US strategic engagement in the entire South Asian region, something to which Washington always aspired but never achieved, since Cold War days up until September 11.

While India was quick to offer the US the use of its military facilities as well as overflight rights for US military operations in Afghanistan in December 2001 (later in Iraq in March 2002) geographic realities made the US choose Pakistan as its frontline state, prompting an Indian foreign ministry official to wonder: "This is absurd. How can the US side with a country that created the Taliban"? New Delhi was concerned when leaders of Western countries visit Islamabad. While India could not be ignored in this war against terror, neither can be Pakistan. India's diplomatic clout has improved, but only in so far as Western anxieties about an escalation of the Kashmir dispute is concerned. It is unclear to what extent India influences American or Western thinking on how to conduct the war on terror globally.

Closer US-India ties have not been at the expense of US Pakistan relations. On the eve of the US-led war on terror, Pakistan emerged, as Raja Mohan put it, both as a part of the problem as well as the solution to the new US security predicament following the September 11 attacks. For a long time, Islamabad created and nurtured an extensive infrastructure in Pakistan that became the breeding ground for all sorts of extremist ideology and groups, including the Taliban. This was partly a by-product of Islamabad's quest for an Islamic identity, which had been undermined by its long association with the United States during the Cold War, and its moderate ideological posture then, that Taliban was propagating. It also closed its eyes when the Taliban movement was hijacked by the Pan Islamic ideology of Osama bin-Laden and made Afghanistan a launching pad for global jihad against the "Jews and the Crusaders".

For Islamabad the September 11 attracks could not have been better timed. Pakistan was getting dangerously close to being declared by the US as a state sponsor of terrorism. With its declining economy, the designation would have cost Islamabad dearly. The country was also on the brink of economic bankruptcy and international isolation. The US-led campaign against the Taliban changed all that. Suddenly Pakistan found the geo-strategic factors weighing heavily in its favour. The United States needed access to the bases that it had helped set up in Pakistan and used during the Soviet occupation of Afghanistan. Alternatively, Washington might have turned to India which from Pakistan's point of view would have been quite damaging. Pakistan's refusal would automatically have legitimized India's long claims on Pakistan's role in sponsoring terrorism in Kashmir. Contrarily, by allying with Washington, Pakistan could camouflage its terrorist leverage against India. Besides, for the US, a campaign in Afghanistan without Pakistan would have been physically and militarily difficult though not impossible. A hostile Islamabad would have undermined the Bush administration is claim that the operation against Taliban was not to be seen as one against Islam.

Access to the bases and the intelligence network in Pakistan also served the other strategic interests of the US other than the ouster of Taliban. For instance, military bases near Dalbandin and Pasni, Baluchistan could be extremely important for the strategic depth they offered with regard to the Gulf region, providing support to the US naval fleet in the Arabian Sea and as an alternative to its bases in Saudi Arabia. For Pakistan as well, co-operation with the US offered wider strategic benefits. Disguised within the framework of mutual cooperation was an implicit assurance that since the US army would be stationed under a broad-based security arrangement in Pakistan it would be hard for India to engage in hot pursuit operations inside Pakistani territory. This was an addition to the US offer of on arms sales, lifting of sanctions imposed against Pakistani nuclear proliferation activities and other forms of military and economic assistance.

Pakistan has offered the Jacobabad, Pasni and Dalbandin air bases to US forces for forward operational purposes. It also allowed the use of Karachi International Airport for the arrival of US military personnel, logistics and for other operations. The American Federal

Bureau of Information has installed monitoring centres at major airports in Pakistan to check passengers. Even Muslims leaving for pilgrimage to Saudi Arabia are being scrutinized on suspicion of being fleeing Al-Qaeda men. In addition, the US is seeking access to close facilities to the Gwadar Port, which Pakistan is developing with Chinese cooperation. This is a strategic site, thanks to its proximity to Afghanistan, Central Asia, and the Gulf. Access to the port could facilitate vital logistics support to US forces in the Arabian Sea.

The US has already agreed to military aid to Pakistan under its Defence Emergency Response Fund for logistical and military support. Pakistan is also eligible for excess parts and equipment from the US army, as are some of the central Asian republics, Egypt and Jordan.

Islamabad's commitment to the US conflicts with the interests of New Delhi just as Pakistan was being isolated internationally. There had been a distinct shift in the US South Asia policy in favour of India especially during the closing years of Clinton Presidency. Washington's Islamabad courtship was almost over. It was chastised for its Kargil misadventure not only by the international community, but even by China. After the September 11 attacks, New Delhi found an opportunity to expose Islamabad as both a perpetrator of and a provider of sanctuary for terrorism. This was important in the context of how Paul Wolfowitz, Deputy Secretary of Defense, set the agenda for the "war on terror" that it not just about "initiating a single military strike or capture a few terrorists and hold them accountable", but also about "removing the sanctuaries, the support systems, ending states" who sponsor terrorism.

But the evolving US-Pakistan security collaboration has dampened the prospects that the US-led global anti-terror campaign would be extended to the Kashmiri militants, many of them backed by Pakistan.

This is not to say that India has not gashed from the US-led war on terror. India's eagerness to help global fight against terrorism "in every possible way" needs be judged in the context of its long-held view that terrorist acts against any one country cannot be seen as problems of that country alone. Besides, for decades India has been on the front line of terror—in Punjab, in Kashmir, in the northeast and even deep in the heartland and down south. For years, New Delhi had been urging the world to institute measures to check terrorism. Although the terrorist camps are located just across the border, India had taken no action due to fear of Pakistani reprisals, which had the potential to turn into a full-scale nuclear war. India also understood that military action against terrorists might not be enough. Action against terrorism, in this context, should be able to dismantle the ideological, military, and financial networks that sustain it.

The December 13, 2001 attacks against the Indian Parliament by groups allegedly operating from Pakistan led to the mobilization of troops by India then by Pakistan in preparation for what appeared to be a major confrontation. Though nothing much happened on the war front, the strategic aerobics on both side of the border was enough to keep the international community on its toes for months. During the entire period however, rhetoric apart, New Delhi earned international commendation for its restraint while a slow but definite pressure was being put on Islamabad to initiate action against the terrorist groups operating from Pakistan. The threat of terrorism also became the catalyst to let New Delhi decisively break out of the isolation caused by its nuclear tests. It was able to reframe the Kashmir issue as one of terrorism. Indo-US ties improved with the US recognition of India as a frontline state in the war against terrorism. This manifested on many fronts, for example, increased democracy and governance assistance, as well as joint patrolling of the strategic Straits of Malacca to guard against threats to shipping. Thus, by playing to American concerns against terrorism, India was able not only to recover strategic clout with the US, vis-à-vis Pakistan, it was also able to make a common cause of the issue of terrorism, especially about the Kashmir insurgency, with the international community.

But India does not and could not fully share the US approach to terror. India's experience with terrorism is fundamentally different from the brand of international terrorism that the US is seeking to eradicate. India is fighting a good number of inbred terrorist groups that are seeking succession from the country, The US, on the other hand, is fighting the terrorists that are waging ideological battles, and which dispire to be a transnational force, rather than a distinctive nation-state.

Islamabad has cooperated with the US under the assumption that its Kashmir policy would continue despite New Delhi's sustained pressure to position Kashmir terrorists as objects of international campaign against terrorism. Even though Washington kept on with pressurizing Islamabad to stop cross border infiltration and clam down on terrorist groups and terrorist networks including training facilities, it might be that the US accepted only a "tactical, operational shift in Pakistan's Kashmir policy". Contrarily, the emerging security volatility in the region made India open up the Kashmir issue for third party mediation and facilitation especially by the US.

Against this backdrop, it is not entirely clear that by shifting to a Curzonian foreign policy, India has enhanced its ability to influence regional and world events. Instead, New Delhi might have got itself circumscribed by a US-centric security framework, one that may also end up according strategic parity to Pakistan. While it may well be worthwhile to keep in mind Curzon's concern for India's territorial and strategic interests, it is equally important to bear in mind that he was an agent of the hegemonic power of the day, able to marshal the vast resources of the empire and put them to use in the service of the "jewel of the crown". Modern Indian leaders do not have this ability and must submit to the whims of the global power structure presently dominated by the US. Hence, India cannot go too far if it uses power politics as the main instrument of its foreign policy approach. Moral politics matters in the Age of Fear, although it need not be particularly Nehruvian. Hence, the view that Curzonian realpolitik would promote Indian interests better than other approaches may be a serious fallacy.

Sources

K.K. Katyal, "Pak. media reports bemoan U.S. role in ministry-making", in *The Hindu*, section: national, November 11, 2002.

Raja Mohan. C. 2003, *Crossing the Rubicon: the shaping of India's new foreign policy*, New Delhi: Viking, India.

"We can help you and you can help us: Bush to PM", in *The Indian Express*, September 17, 2001, New Delhi.

28

Howard's Corollary

By openly endorsing Australia's Prime Minister, John Howard's call for pre-emptive strikes against terrorist havens in Southeast Asia, the Bush administration may be harming its own relationships in Asia and its war on terror in the region. Imitation is the highest form of flattery, they say. Bush might be pleased to see Howard, already known for his willingness to be "deputy sheriff" to the US in Southeast Asia, articulate a strategic policy echoing the infamous Bush Doctrine on pre-emption. But there are important costs to both Washington and Canberra.

The exact nature of the Howard policy remains to be clarified, especially whether the military action it envisages would be unilateral or in cooperation with governments of the concerned states. If unilateralism is an option, then the Howard corollary actually goes a step further than Bush's pre-emptive strategy. The latter targets "rogue" states accused of developing weapons of mass destruction and exporting terror. Howard's targets are Southeast Asian states who have no plan for such weapons and who are not willing exporters of terror to Australia or elsewhere.

Why such a policy now? The obvious factor is the perceived terrorist threat to Australia, starkly underscored by the Bali tragedy. Howard feels that domestic political considerations would prevent Asian governments, especially Indonesia, from accepting Australia's help in rooting out terrorists on their soil plotting against Australian interests. Hence Australia must have its own pre-emptive strategy.

But Howard is known in Asia for being a staunch, if politically insecure nationalist. His pro-US stance in the wake of the Bali tragedy, with pre-emptive regional strikes, can be expected to appeal to a domestic audience questioning the government's preparedness against terror and demanding stern action against the Al-Qaeda network. And Howard has never been known to be unduly sensitive to Asian opinion.

After taking the reins of power, Howard downgraded his Labour predecessor Paul Keating's close engagement with Asia and strengthened defence links with the US. He strengthened Australia's security ties with the US, in keeping with its traditional security strategy of defending its interests in Asia and beyond in close collaboration with "great and powerful friends". Southeast Asians are obviously neither great nor powerful enough to be courted as strategic partners as Howard moves Australia from forward defence to forward pre-emption.

Against this backdrop, some criticisms of Howard are legitimate, especially his failure to consult with Asian countries before taking a major strategic leap of faith. Indeed, with vision and diplomacy, Howard could have developed a joint strategy for preventive military and political action against regional terrorists with the full support and participation of his Asian neighbours.

Absent such backing, the Howard posture could become counterproductive by provoking Asian anger and making Asian governments unwilling to cooperate with Australian security forces against the common threat of terrorism. It could alienate Australia's Asian immigrant community. It may even prompt some Asian governments or rogue elements in their security forces to deliberately let terrorist threats to Australia unattended, thereby rendering the Howard policy a self-fulfilling prophecy.

Yet, there need be no overreaction to the Howard corollary.

Australia lacks the capacity for significant distant intervention, especially when undertaken unilaterally. More importantly, Howard is by no means riding on a national consensus. On the contrary, some of his severest critics of his statement have been the Australian media and his Labour opponents at home.

In the meantime, the Howard statement signifies the sad disappearance of the energetic and ingenuous Australian diplomacy which in the early 1990s played an instrumental role in the development of regional cooperation in the form of Asia Pacific Economic Cooperation and the ASEAN Regional Forum. Under Hawke, Keating and Evans, Canberra's ideas and initiatives were regarded in Asia as well-meaning, internationalist and independent-minded (from the US). Today, the same country, albeit under a different government, makes news in an entirely different manner, not by rising above domestic chauvinism and opposing American unilateralism, but by pandering to narrow nationalist sentiments and uncritically backing a questionable US strategy.

29

An Opportunity for Global Order Reform

Major wars always bring with them an opportunity for reforming and rebuilding international order. The war in the Gulf may be one such opportunity.

The first opportunity is for Security Council reform. Australian Prime Minister John Howard, one of America's staunchest allies, has called for expanding the UN Security Council with a slew of new permanent members without the veto power. Among the countries he has proposed for these slots are Japan, Indonesia and India.

If Howard is serious, and there is no indication that he may be so inclined in restoring the health of the global multilateral system, his proposal has considerable merit. Security Council reform has languished for decades in UN committees and academic circles. Getting Japan, India and Indonesia into the Council will strengthen Asian voices in the body in which China is the only permanent Asian member to date. Japan is Asia's most advanced industrial nation and among the world's largest donors of development assistance. India and Indonesia are developing nations. Together with Japan, they share a commitment to democracy. India is the largest democracy in the world. Indonesia is the largest Muslim nation. According it a permanent Council seat will send a powerful signal at a time when the West and the US need to reach out to Islamic societies. It will also advance the cause of democracy.

Both India and Indonesia are leaders of the Third World. Both have behaved responsibly in dealing with regional security challenges. Indonesia was responsible for the creation of ASEAN and remains a constructive regional actor with its post-Bali crackdown on transnational terrorism. India has shown restraint with its nuclear weapon capability by renouncing first use. India's recent peace overtures to Pakistan will help its claim to Council membership and be further encouraged by it. Japan has shown restraint in dealing with North Korea and shown an unfailing commitment to peaceful ways of diffusing and managing periodic crises in the Korean peninsula.

A second task requiring the urgent attention of the international community is to develop new rules for undertaking humanitarian intervention. The post-Cold War idea of humanitarian intervention emerged in no place other than Iraq in 1991 when US-led coalition forces offered protection to Kurdish people from further vengeance by the Saddam regime.

In the 2003 Gulf War, the human rights of the Iraqi people was not the prime motivation. To quote White House Press Secretary Ari Fleischer, the Iraqi possession of weapons of mass destruction "is what this war was and is about".

President Bush and his supporters have pointed to the "cheering crowds" of Baghdad as the ultimate vindication of their quick and decisive victory. But there is an irony here.

Members of America's "coalition of the willing" may not necessarily support the idea of humanitarian intervention out of concern that it will undermine state sovereignty. And many nations who criticised the Iraq war and stayed out of the US-led coalition are among the staunchest proponents of humanitarian intervention, including France and Canada. It was the French Foreign Minister who in 1991 asserted the international community's "right to intervene" to alleviate human suffering caused by repression, civil disorder, inter-state conflict and natural disasters. And Canada, which participated in past interventions in Iraq, Bosnia and Kosovo, sponsored the International Commission on Intervention and State Sovereignty, with a mandate to make humanitarian intervention more "legitimate and efficient".

The commission, chaired by the former Australian Foreign Minister Gareth Evans and Mohamed Sahnoun of Alegria, produced a report, entitled *Responsibility to Protect*, a clever and useful twist to "right to intervene". The report reflects the consensus of commissioners drawn from all regions, religions and civilizations of the world.

It recommends that humanitarian intervention should be undertaken only in extreme cases, such as the large-scale violation of human rights and ethnic cleansing. It argues against the use of humanitarian intervention for geopolitical or strategic interests of any country.

The report does not rule out a "coalition of the willing" approach if the Security Council reacts too slowly or fails to act. But it does insist that the work of such coalitions be consistent with the specified criteria, meaning that intervention is justified only as a "last resort", if its employs "proportional means" against the level of abuses committed, has "reasonable prospects" of success, and above all, is undertaken with the "right intention", underscoring the need to limit intervention to acute humanitarian crises only.

Unfortunately, the release of the report coincided with the September 11 attacks on the United States. But the post-war uncertainty about the future of the UN makes it opportune to start a discussion of its message and recommendations.

If the Gulf War was really about human suffering, then there can be nothing more urgent than seeking new ideas about how the international community can handle future Iraqs without holding the entire multilateral system to hostage. And there is no other document which provides a better and more practical blueprint for achieving this goal than the *Responsibility to Protect*.

Sources

"Australian PM backs five for Security Council permanent states", BBC Monitoring Asia-Pacific: political supplied by BBC worldwide monitoring, April 30, 2003.

Ganeth Evans and Mohamed Sahnoun, "The Responsibility to Protect", in Foreign Affairs, section: essay, p. 99, November–December 2002.

30

Waging the "War on Terror": Singapore's Responses and Dilemmas

The war on terror, launched and spearheaded by the United States in response to the catastrophic attacks on the World Trade Center and the Pentagon on September 11, 2001, has presented the international community with difficult choices. On the one hand, the threat posed by terrorism to world peace and stability is universally recognized, especially by those states which themselves are facing this menace. In the aftermath of the September 11 attacks, the US drew worldwide sympathy and promises of cooperation from nations across continents and civilizations in its quest to punish the perpetrators. On the other hand, the international community remains sharply polarized over aspects of the war on terror waged by the Bush administration. Three elements of the US response have proven to be especially divisive. The first is the Bush administration's penchant for unilateral action. The second is the Bush doctrine of pre-emption. The third is the attack on Iraq, which the Bush administration initially justified by citing Iraq's alleged possession of weapons of mass destruction—a justification which has not been backed by credible evidence even after the US victory in Iraq.

Despite its overarching nomenclature, there is no single "war of terror". The latter is a continuing multi-dimensional and multifront effort; some aspects of which enjoy greater legitimacy in the international community than others. In the past year, Singapore has been involved in two important facets of the war on terror. The first is its effort to disrupt and destroy the Jemaah Islamiah (JI) network and protect Singapore from potential terrorist attacks. The second is to respond to US expectations for support from its allies for the war to effect regime change in Iraq, a war which Washington has presented to the international community as an integral part of its war on terror. While the first challenge was operationally more demanding, the second has proved to be politically challenging.

Singapore's Anti-Terror Efforts

Although terrorism had been recognized as a danger to Singapore before the September 11 attacks, there was clearly no sense of its magnitude prior to the attacks. As Prime Minister Goh Chok Tong put it:

> We knew that it could be a problem, but we did not know the size of it. We knew that there were local organizations which were prepared to use terror against the governments, but we thought they were regional, local. We did not know they were tied up with Al-Qaeda.

The arrest since late 2001 of 31 men believed to be JI members seeking to bomb the US embassy and other foreign missions, as well as local targets put Singapore on the global map of terrorist targets. The Bali bombings in October 2002 heightened the sense of vulnerability to the JI terrorist network.

In the 2003, Singapore intensified its counter-terrorism drive. In February, DPM Tony Tan urged Singaporeans to be "psychologically prepared" for a terrorist attack. He pointed to Singapore's "high visibility as a target" for groups like Al-Qaeda and JI. And the joint statement between PM Goh and President Bush during the latter's visit to Singapore in October 2003 recognized that while "much headway had been made in disrupting terrorist networks ... more needed to be done and that the campaign against terrorism required a sustained long-term effort".

What has been this "sustained long-term effort"? Singapore's overall response to terrorism may be divided into three areas: homeland security, bilateral cooperation and regional measures.

Singapore's approach to homeland security seeks to ensure greater inter-ministerial coordination, improve sharing of intelligence, and enhance its capacity for joint action involving civilian and military forces in countering terrorism. Among the steps undertaken are:

- The establishment of a special committee to oversee airport security.
- "Hardening" of key infrastructure and installations like the Jurong Island, with its many petrochemical companies against terrorist attacks.

- Intensified security measures to protect more public areas, such as Holland Village and Boat Quay.
- Strengthened border controls, such as full checks on all vehicles, passengers and baggage at border checkpoints with Malaysia.
- Exercising contingency plans for scenarios such as major fires and bomb explosions.
- Security briefings for target audiences such as security managers of commercial buildings, owners of entertainment outlets and grassroot organizations.
- The creation of Community, Safety and Security Programmes (CSSP) for the general public which bring together residents, grassroots leaders and neighbourhood police officers to identify and deal with potential security problems.
- Deployment of air marshals on Singapore Airlines flights in an effort to forestall possible hijackings and terror attacks.

Singapore is the first port in Asia to participate in the Container Security Initiative, which allows US inspectors to check cargo bound for US destinations for possible shipments of explosives or weapons of mass destruction. The US and Singapore cooperate closely in intelligence-sharing. Bilateral tensions have not precluded intelligence-sharing between Singapore and its neighbours against terrorist groups. In October, during the Bush visit, the two countries announced their decision to work towards a "Framework Agreement for the Promotion of a Strategic Cooperation Partnership in Defense and Security". This would expand bilateral cooperation in counterterrorism, counterproliferation of weapons of mass destruction, joint military exercises and training, policy dialogues, and defense technology.

On the multilateral front, Singapore is a party to the ASEAN-United States of America Joint Declaration for Cooperation To Combat International Terrorism, which seeks to create "a framework for cooperation to prevent, disrupt and combat international terrorism through the exchange and flow of information, intelligence and capacity-building".

At the regional level, Singapore works within the framework of ASEAN, the ASEAN Regional Forum (ARF) and the Asia-Pacific Economic Cooperation (APEC) to combat terrorism. Some of the initiatives undertaken by these organizations include:

- Promoting common adherence to international conventions on terrorism and integrating them with ASEAN mechanisms;
- Calling for the early signing/ratification of or accession to anti-terrorist conventions;
- Designating Principal Contact Points in all ASEAN member countries on counter-terrorism (CT);
- Holding meetings of ASEAN Police Chiefs to discuss practical measures and explore avenues of cooperation against terrorism;
- Increasing cooperation among front-line law enforcement agencies in combating terrorism and sharing "best practices";
- Providing for greater exchange of information/intelligence on terrorists and terrorist organizations, their movement and funding, and other information needed to protect lives, property and the security of all modes of travel;
- Development of regional capacity building programmes to enhance existing capabilities of ASEAN member countries to investigate, detect, monitor and report on terrorist acts;
- The ARF Agreement on Measures Against Terrorist Financing.

Regional cooperation on counter-terrorism remains constrained by divergent national priorities, lingering bilateral disputes and unequal national security capabilities. Hence, Singapore sees regional cooperation as a complement to national and bilateral efforts, rather than a substitute.

The War Over Iraq

The forced regime change in Iraq is particularly damaging to world order because the most principled criticisms of the US action comes from America's allies in the developed West, rather than its usual detractors in the Third World. The belated US justification of the war as a humanitarian effort to rid Iraqi people of a murderous regime has not been convincing, given that the war was initially presented as a counter to Iraq's alleged possession of weapons of mass destruction.

In contrast to Europe, where the war created a major split within NATO, America's allies in Asia have generally closed ranks with the US. Expediency and pragmatism, stemming from security dependence on the US in the face of continuing geopolitical threats and a traditional faith in the US-led regional balance of power order, have outweighed considerations of principles at stake in the weakening of the multilateral order. All the treaty allies of the US—Japan, South Korea, Philippines and Thailand—found reasons of "national interest" to back the US attack on Iraq. Singapore, though not a party to the San Francisco system of alliances, has followed the same course, basing its decision on the exigencies of its national interest.

A week before the war, in remarks before the Parliament on March 14, the Foreign Minister S. Jayakumar indicated that Singapore's stance on Iraq would be guided by the issue of Iraqi compliance with UN Security Council resolutions calling for its immediate disarmament. If there was to be "a use of force, it must be because of Iraq's failure to comply".

On the question of whether Singapore was being too pro-US, he responded that Singapore was neither pro-US nor "anti-any country", but simply "being pro-Singapore". While Singapore "strongly advocate[s] US's continued presence and engagement in this region" and has "excellent bilateral relations with the US ... that does not mean that we are subservient to the US or that we agree with everything that the US does, or says, or requests, without regard to our own national interests".

While Singapore neither received nor needed the kind of financial inducements from America that might have lured others into the "coalition of the willing", the fact that the war came at a critical final stage of negotiations of the US-Singapore free trade agreement was not lost on observers. It is noteworthy that Singapore has not sought "major non-NATO ally" status that Thailand and the Philippines currently enjoy with the US.

Two days after the US launched its invasion of Iraq on March 20, 2003, Deputy Prime Minister Tony Tan declared that it "will allow US aircraft to fly over Singapore ... allow US military assets and ships and aircraft to call at Singapore to use our military bases. We have made these facilities available to the US during this campaign as we did in the campaign in Afghanistan".

Singapore permitted the US to be named as a member of the "coalition of the willing". Later, after the US victory in Iraq, Singapore would dispatch 192 Singapore Armed Forces (SAF) personnel to provide logistics support for the Iraqi reconstruction.

A specific justification for Singapore's support for the US was voiced by the Minister for Trade and Industry George Yeo during a trip to the US to promote the bilateral free trade agreement. According to Yeo, "Singapore supported the US on Iraq because it recognized that US leadership is indispensable in the world today, especially in the war against global terrorism. If Saddam Hussein could thumb his nose at the US, other rogue governments and organizations would have been encouraged to create mischief as well".

This seemed to stress the need to protect US credibility, rather than implying concurrence with the Bush administration's stated justifications for the attack, which centred on ridding Iraq weapons of mass destruction.

PM Goh Chok Tong himself stressed the dangers posed by Iraq's attempt to acquire weapons of mass destruction as the basis for Singapore's support for regime change in Iraq. "It is clear to everyone, unless that person wears blinkers, that this is a war to remove the weapons of mass destruction from Saddam Hussein". Singapore had to support the US because "if weapons of mass destruction were to fall into the hands of terrorists, they could also become a threat to Singapore, which two years ago was targeted by a terrorist group".

What Goh did not specify, of course, was whether in Singapore's view Saddam was in actual possession of such weapons. This made his stance different from Tony Blair, who had insisted on intelligence information pointing to Iraqi possession of such weapons which could be deployed at very short notice.

(Subsequently, as the failure of occupying US forces to find any credible evidence of an active Iraqi programme to acquire weapons of mass destruction fuelled an international controversy over the war's purpose, the Foreign Ministry reacted strongly to a commentary in the *Straits Times* questioning the government's support for the US. On June 11, Foreign Ministry spokeswoman Tan Lian Choo said in a letter to the newspaper that the search for the weapons was "still ongoing" and nobody at this point in time can say conclusively that there were no WMD in Iraq. Singapore was "not embarrassed" by the US failure to find WMD so far, and had taken a "strong, principled and consistent position on Iraq based on Singapore's national interests". Tan concluded by saying that Singaporeans "cannot afford to strike postures fashionable with the oppositionist media in America and Britain at the expense of the security of Singaporeans" and that "a small nation in terrorist-infested Southeast Asia does not have this luxury of libertarian posturing".)

Goh's invoking of the weapons of mass destruction was to stress the strategic rationale for the war, at a time when the war was being perceived by sections of the Muslim population as being an anti-Islam crusade. Hence his assertion that the war was about getting rid of Iraq's weapons of mass destruction was apparently designed to underscore the point before Singapore's Muslim populations that this "is not an Islamic issue, or a case of the West trying to hit out at Islam".

While Singapore is a significant beneficiary of its cooperation with the US in coping with transnational terror, the war on terror is not without costs for Singapore's security and political interests, costs which are not lost to the government. One such cost has to do with the spill-over effect of the growing anti-Americanism in Singapore's neighbourhood. Tony Tan acknowledged this when he warned on January 4, 2004 that Singapore is a prize target for terrorists because of its support for the US war on terror.

A second cost was alluded to by PM Goh in his speech to the Asia Society on May 7, 2003, when he acknowledged that "the Iraq War…has raised grave questions about the future of the UN." Considering that UN has been recognized by Singapore's foreign policymakers as a bulwark of the sovereignty of small states, a significant weakening of this institution cannot but be detrimental to the republic's strategic interests.

The divisive effect of the war on international order and dangers posed by rising anti-Americanism to the interests of America's allies were clearly articulated by Senior Minister Lee Kuan Yew. Speaking at the 2nd Shangri-la Dialogue in May 2003, Lee warned that "Throughout history, every force has generated a counter-force". While "Russia, China and many countries in the European Union want to maintain good or friendly relations with the United States", if the US was to ignore their feelings, this will "persuade more nations that the way to restrain American unilateralism is to join a group of all those opposed to it".

Lee's advice to the US against unilateralism was grounded not on idealist principles of international conduct. Rather, it derived from the core assumptions of realism, which believes in the tendency of absolute power to invite countervailing responses from rival powers and coalitions. While other Southeast Asians, such as the Prime Minister Mahathir of Malaysia, had criticized the US for neglecting the root causes of terror and doing little to address the unjust suffering of the Palestinians, Lee's comment was significant as it came from a long-standing ally of America with a reputation for clear-eyed realpolitik. This was perhaps a more telling warning against the long-term dangers posed by American unilateralism that might damage the interests not just of the hegemon itself, but also that of its allies like Singapore.

Sources

ASEAN-United States of America Joint Declaration for Cooperation To Combat International Terrorism, Bandar Seri Begawan, Brunei, August 1, 2002.

http://www.aseansec.org/14396.htm.

http://www.aseansec.org/15133.htm.

http://www.aseansec.org/14396.htm.

"Bush talks terror with Singapore leaders," *USA Today*, 10/21/2003.

http://www.usatoday.com/news/world/2003-10-21-bush-asia_x.htm.

Online Newshour, May 7, 2003, http://www.pbs.org/newshour/bb/asia/jan-june03/goh_05-07-03.html.

http://usinfo.state.gov/topical/pol/terror/texts/03102107.htm.

http://www.pbs.org/newshour/bb/asia/jan-june03/goh_05-07-03.html.

"Koizumi, Goh agree on U.N. role in postwar Iraq," *Asian Political News*, March 31, 2003.

http://www.findarticles.com/cf_dls/m0WDQ/2003_March_31/99448274/p1/article.jhtml' "After Iraq", Address by Senior Minister Lee Kuan Yew to the 2nd Shangri-La Dialogue, May 30–June 1, 2003.

"Moderate Muslims know goal in Iraq: PM Goh", *Straits Times*, March 29, 2003. http://straitstimes.asia1.com.sg/iraqwar/story/0,4395,179932,00.html.

Remarks in Parliament by Singapore Foreign Minister Prof S Jayakumar on Strategic Review in the World, Including the Situation in Iraq, and Asia-Pacific Region, March 14, 2003.

http://www.mfa.gov.sg/iraq.html#Iraq.

See also "Singapore defends support for war on Iraq, says weapons search not over".

Speech by Trade and Industry Minister George Yeo at the US Chamber of Commerce on April 28, 2003.

http://app10.internet.gov.sg/scripts/mfa/pr/admin ussfta_list_title_SGdisplay.asp?View,15.

Singapore, Agence France Presse, June 11, 2003.

"Singapore ups spending for defence, homeland security", Singapore, Agence France Presse, February 28, 2003.

"Singapore: support for US makes it top terror target", Agence France-Presse, May 24, 2003.

"Singapore ups spending for defence, homeland security", Singapore, Agence France Presse, February 28, 2003. http://www.singapore-window.org/sw03/030228a1.htm.

"S'pore lays out plans to beat airline terrorists", *Straits Times*, January 4, 2004, http://straitstimes.asia1.com.sg/topstories/story/0,4386,228460-1073339940,00.html.

http://www.asiasociety.org/speeches/tong03.html.

Tan Lian Choo, letter to the Editor, "Singapore's support for action on Iraq prompted by wider concerns", *Straits Times*, June 11, 2003.

Tan Tarn How, "No sign of Iraqi weapons: How now, Singapore?", *Straits Times*, June 7, 2003.

Epilogue

Indeed, since the war in Iraq, our role as a force for stability has deteriorated in virtually every trouble spot. Syria, the Palestinians, North Korea, Iran—where there has been a change in America's ability to work for a reduction in violence, tension, and instability, it has been for the worse.

US Congressman Barney Frank, October 10, 2003

31

When the War Was (Not) Over

On May 1, 2003, President George W. Bush flew in a S-3B Viking from a naval base in San Diego to the aircraft carrier USS Abraham Lincoln anchored in the Pacific Ocean, he became the first sitting US president to accomplish a "tailhook" landing. It was a close shave. The presidential jet managed to catch the last of the four steel wires across the flight deck positioned to help the plane land on the aircraft carrier. Failure to do so would have plunged the S-3B into the Pacific Ocean waters off the California coast. Once on the deck, Bush proclaimed: "Major combat operations in Iraq have ended. In the battle of Iraq, the United States and our allies have prevailed. And now our coalition is engaged in securing and reconstructing that country".

A few days later, I submitted an op-ed piece to a local newspaper on the various debates surrounding the Iraq war (which appears in this volume as "Making Sense of the Gulf War Debate"). I received a prompt and polite reply from the op-ed editor on the same evening: "Hi Amitav ... the topic sounds a bit outdated from a newspaper point of view—it would have been great if we have this shortly after war ended. Are you not planning a wider piece on American foreign policy"?

Aghast, I promptly replied: "I am not sure the war has 'ended'". The editor responded: "I have read the piece, personally I like it but ... I still feel it is a bit outdated in a sense since it focuses on the Iraqi debate, which in my view, has shifted to many other things. So [I] won't be able to use the piece ... Actually I am interested ... about American foreign policy in post-Iraq war. Are you planning anything along those lines?"

I thought of firing off an angry response, but then thought better of it. Anger will get you nowhere, especially if you want to make future submissions. Instead, I started writing the piece that the editor had wanted, focusing on the Bush administration's "post-Iraq" foreign policy. I did have my revenge, however. When the piece was completed, I sent it to a rival paper (which published it under "How Will Mr Bush Run the World?". Despite this concession to pragmatism and pride, I remained convinced that the "war had not ended".

I was, as it turned out, on solid ground. Among the many people who would agree with my view was President Bush himself. And not just Bush, but also Paul Wolfowitz, CNN, Fox News, fringe suburban peace movements and, of course, fellow academics.

But they agreed for different reasons. And therein lies a tale, a tale not just about the causes of the Iraq War, but also of its consequences for Iraq's and our future.

Despite his brave feat, Bush was not proclaiming the war to be over. "Difficult work remained to be done in Iraq." Comparing the speech with his father's televised words in February 1991 after Saddam had been kicked out of Kuwait, veteran political commentator Bill Schneider noted that while George Sr. had called his a "war" ("The war is now behind us".) aboard the Abraham Lincoln, George Jr. would only call his a "battle" ("The battle of Iraq is one victory in a war on terror that began on September 11, 2001, and still goes on".).

On October 17, the President reiterated this theme. He said that he was not ready to declare victory in Iraq or end the fighting even though Saddam Hussein is "no longer in power". "I want to hear our commanders say we have achieved the clear objectives that we have set out. That's when we will say this is over," the President said. He reflected further on the progress in Iraq. "We've had an historic week", he said. "I don't think I'll ever forget, I'm sure a lot of other people will never forget the statue of Saddam Hussein falling in Baghdad and then seeing the jubilation on the faces of ordinary Iraqis as they realised that the grip of fear that had them by the throat had been released, the first signs of freedom".

Such jubilation did not, however extend to other nations, including allied ones. Weeks after the war, I took part in a public forum in Singapore. Someone asked the speakers and audience to raise hands if they supported the war. Out of about 200 people in the room, only about two hands went up: an American and a British diplomat. The overwhelming rejection of the war almost made you rebellious, to support the war if not for anything, but to be different.

But the Bush administration was fighting victory. An opportunity for bringing the UN to help with nation-building was rebuffed. The administration abandoned its road map for Palestine which offered a way to legitimize the victory. Bush's critics agreed with him that the war was not over yet, but something else was also not over yet: misinformation about the war's cause and cost.

In an September 8 article subtitled "The War in Iraq is Not Over and Neither Are the Lies to Justify It", academic Stephen Zunes took issue with Bush over the weapons of mass destruction saga. A day earlier, Bush had proclaimed: "Two years ago, I told the Congress and the country that the war on terror would be a lengthy war, a different kind of war, fought on many fronts in many places. Iraq is now the central front".

Rendering Iraq as the "central front" in the war on terror should be regarded as the Iraq War's singular achievement. Before the war, terrorism experts, including those favoured by Western governments, had clearly dismissed any link between Al-Qaeda and Saddam. Rohan Gunaratna, whom no one can accuse of being soft on terrorism, argued that not only was there no link between Saddam and Al-Qaeda, but that the attack on Iraq could actually harm and rather than help the war on terror.

Later, on September 16, Bush would himself concede that he had no evidence that Saddam was involved in September 11 attacks. He refuted Cheney, who would only say "we don't know" when asked about the link. But, Bush added, "There's no question that Saddam Hussein had Al-Qaeda ties".

Many Americans believed that some of the hijackers were Iraqi, when none were, and that the attacks had been orchestrated by Baghdad, despite any concrete evidence to support that. About a year earlier, in August 2002, Alex Standish, editor of the UK journal *Jane's Intelligence Digest*—required reading for war-watchers and war-makers everywhere—thinks US intelligence officials are making "a big mistake" on Iraq. "The idea that Al-Qaeda is getting political or military support from Iraq is ludicrous. I can see no way".

Yet, sadly enough, what the Al-Qaeda could not manage during Saddam's reign, it got when Paul Bremer took over. Now Iraq has a Saddam-Osama duet, with each competing with the other to make appearances on Al-Jazeera and outdoing the other in exhorting Iraqis to ensure that the war continues. Terrorist attacks, such as that of the UN Headquarters that killed Sergei Viera De Mello and that on the Al-Rasheed Hotel that nearly killed Wolfowitz, bear the stamp of Al-Qaeda in terms of their close coordination and suicide tactics.

Terrorism was, of course, not the main justification for the war. It was the WMDs stupid. When confronted with the issue that the US troops combing Iraq for these weapons confessed to failure, Bush officials tried different tactics. While Tony Blair kept insisting that he had "absolutely no doubt" that concrete evidence will be found of Saddam's weapons of mass destruction, and advised reporters to "have a little patience". Bush's chief hawk, US Deputy Secretary of Defense Paul Wolfowitz, admitted to a different rationale for stressing the WMD angle. He said in an interview with *Vanity Fair*, May 9, 2003: "For bureaucratic reasons we settled on one issue, weapons of mass destruction, because it was the one reason everyone could agree on". (The Pentagon transcript of the interview was slightly different: "The truth is that for reasons that have a lot to do with the US government bureaucracy, we settled on the one issue that everyone could agree on which was weapons of mass destruction as the core reason".

Ultimately, what might save Bush-Blair is a belief that they might simply have been mistaken, but have not deliberately misled the American public. Wolfowitz insists that Saddam's alleged weapons of mass destruction were an important and legitimate reason for the war. He insists that "there have always been three fundamental concerns". "One is weapons of mass destruction, the second is support for terrorism, the third is the criminal treatment of the Iraqi people". A fourth, he added, was the removal of a "cause of instability" in the Middle East. (Yet, in the same interview, Wolfowitz complicated matters by hinting at a fifth rationale for the war, the removal of US troops from Saudi Arabia. An "almost unnoticed—but it's huge" outcome of the war, he insisted, was that it removed the need to maintain American forces in Saudi Arabia as long as Saddam was in power. *Vanity Fair* interpreted Wolfowitz statement as saying that the withdrawal of US troops from Saudi Arabia was one major reason for going to war, rather than just an outcome.)

Wolfowitz himself is, of course, a key member of the "war is not over" camp, at least if one is to believe a column in the liberal-minded *Washington Post*. In "'Wolfowitz's War': Not Over Yet", appearing on May 13, 2003, David Ignatius reported that "Even on the day that Saddam Hussein's statue toppled in Baghdad just over a month ago, Paul Wolfowitz says he allowed himself only a "tempered emotion" of victory. "Symbolically, it was not unlike seeing the Berlin Wall come down. It's one of those images that will stand". Wolfowitz confirmed his view on the fateful day of October 27, just after his hotel (Al-Rasheed) in Baghdad was attacked by rockets. An editorial in the *Straits Times* of Singapore on October 28 entitled "Iraq war not over" reported a "shaken but unhurt Deputy Defence Secretary Paul Wolfowitz, who escaped down a stairwell past thickening smoke" telling reporters that Iraq remained a danger zone "as long as there are criminals out there staging hit-and-run attacks".

The war is also not over for America's neighbourhood peace groups. Consider the group known as the Watts/South Gate Youth. Their campaign, titled: "The war is not over!!!" begins by reminding the reader of the definition of war.

> War (wôr) n. 1. Armed conflict between nations, states, or factions. 2. A determined struggle esp. For a specific goal. 3. A state of antagonism or discord. 4. Military techniques or procedures as a science.

According to this group, "War does not stop when the last bomb is dropped. War stops when people create a lasting peace based on justice and equality. No justice, no peace! Don't believe the T.V. hype, the war's not over!"

To speak of media hype during the war immediately brings to mind three things: the "embedded" American journalist, Saddam's information minister Muhammed Saeed al-Sahaf and Rupert Murdoch's Fox News. The embedding of the media is the most significant advance in military strategy in our times. It did wonders for Rumsfeld's image as a military genius (can an embedded journalist write anything negative about the troops when his life remains in their hands?)

The Iraqi information minister, also known simply as MSS, refused to the let the Americans win (and thereby end) the war even after coalition forces had captured Saddam Hussein International Airport: "Today we slaughtered them in the airport. They are out of Saddam International Airport". When the Army dashed into the heart of Baghdad, MSS blurted: "There are only two American tanks in the city", and "I triple guarantee you, there are no American soldiers in Baghdad". The same man who claimed to "speak better English than this villain Bush" (not as outrageous a boast as it might seem), and assured skeptics that "lying is forbidden in Iraq" because "President Saddam Hussein…is a man of great honour and integrity", endeared himself to people the world over, including, it seems, the occupying forces, who allowed him to slip out of Iraq.

The question of when the Iraqi war would be over also brings to mind Fox News, the chief propaganda channel for the neo-cons. On April 18, 2003, Steven Milloy of Fox News wrote: "The war in Iraq is pretty much over, except for junk scientists. For them, the war may continue for decades–just like Vietnam". He was reacting, among others, to a report by the United Nations Environment Program (UNEP) that it would investigate allegations that coalition forces used armour-piercing weapons containing depleted uranium (DU). These radioactive weapons are highly injurious to health and could implicate the coalition for using cruel and inhuman methods. Milloy compares this investigation to the controversy about the use of Agent Orange in Vietnam. He cites a new study published in the journal *Nature* which argues that the amount of this chemical agent used was significantly underestimated and called for more study of US troops and Vietnamese civilians in the sprayed areas. Just as Agent Orange kept the Vietnam War from being over, worried Milloy, so could the depleted uranium issue in brining closure to the Iraq war.

Inadvertently, Fox News brought up the issue of human suffering caused by the war. According to a group called *Iraqi Body Count* (iraqbodycount.net), the US invasion led to between 2,233 and 2,706 Iraqi civilian deaths. The number of Iraqi soldiers ("mostly poor conscripts compelled to fight") who lost their lives could be in tens of thousands. Another estimate (www.commondreams.org) puts Iraqi civilian deaths at more than 5,000 and reminds the reader that the number far surpasses "the number of American civilians killed in the terrorist attacks of 9/11". The Project on Defence Alternatives, as reported by *The Economist*, suggests that between 10,800 and 15,100 Iraqis were killed, including some 3,200 to 4,300 non-combatants.

CNN also does not take the war to be over. As its political commentator Bill Schneider noted: "War not over as 2004 campaign begins". While the previous Saddam war was all but forgotten in the 1992 presidential campaign, the Bush Jr. administration "is determined not to let the war slip off the campaign agenda". At least that was the case in May 2003.

Other reasons why the war is not over in Iraq have to do with resistance and reconstruction. Here too, the Watts/South Gate Youth is pretty authoritative. "There is still war in Iraq" not just because "the Iraqi people continue to fight", but "also we [America] still have to rebuild Iraq".

The issue of Iraqi resistance is quite mystifying in many ways. Before the war, most people worried about the fighting capacity of the Republican Guards in an urban environment. But Saddam's elite forces bolted and "melted" into the civilian population. The less regular militia "Fedayeen" caused so much trouble for advancing coalition forces that the commander of US forces in Iraq, General William Wallace, candidly confessed that the war his forces was fighting in Iraq was not the war they had "war-gamed" against. There was a moment of hope that the Fedayeen might put a spanner on Rumsfeld's "shock and awe" campaign. This did not happen, but this was the beginning of suicide attacks on coalition forces. This also presaged Saddam's ability to turn this war and the occupation into a guerrilla campaign.

Other assumptions made by the Rumsfeld team about how to end the war now seem to be deeply flawed. There was no mass uprising in Iraq as the US troops marched towards Baghdad. Coalition soldiers were not welcomed by hordes of flag-waving, cheering Iraqis, even the Shiites in southern Iraq. Even Coalition humanitarian supplies have been met by angry crowds. The war has rekindled the deeply ingrained aversion in the Arab mind to foreign intimidation and occupation.

But Rumsfeld cannot be blamed for declaring the war to be over prematurely, even as he witnessed the single most vivid image of Coalition triumph in Iraq. On April 9, 2003 an event produced and directed by the embedded media with the help of US forces (hence the epithets "mother of all photo ops" and "Topplegate") a US Marine tow truck accomplished what Iraqis (so impoverished by the Saddam regime that they could only find a noose and a single sledgehammer as equipment) could not do for the past few days. They brought down the 20-foot (or was it 40-foot?) statue of Saddam Hussein on Baghdad's al-Fardos (Paradise) Square. "A frenzied mob roared and jumped and danced on the fallen statue," as America's ABC news put it.

It mattered little that, these people were not citizens of Baghdad. The jubilant Iraqis were members of the United States-based Iraqi National Congress, whose leader Ahmed Chalabi stands a chance of being the next president of Iraq.

Time's James Poniewozik put it well: "Was it amazing that we saw a war's climax live on TV? Or did this become the war's climax because it happened live on TV? After that statue of the tyrant fell, it was irresistible, if wrong, to speak of the war in the past tense. Fighting is a physical state; war, in the absence of formal declarations and surrenders, is a state of mind. The battle might drag on bloodily for months. But this moment—hollow Saddam collapsing, his metal insides jutting out—was too perfect, too cinematic, for the war not to be over".

The event was beamed by satellite worldwide. Among those watching was Bush, who called the event something he would never forget because it sparked so much "jubilation on the faces of ordinary Iraqis as they realized that the grip of fear that had them by the throat had been released". According to White House spokesman Ari Fleischer, President Bush watching the statue fall on television, said, "They got it down". "The president is filled with joy for the fact that the Iraqi people soon will be free", Fleischer added. Yet for Rumsfeld, the war was still "not over". "There is a lot more fighting that is going to be done", Rumsfeld said. "There are more people going to be killed, let there be no doubt. This is not over despite all the celebrations in the streets".

And how right he was. Just when no one thought it was safe to return to the streets of Baghdad, the resistance reappeared. The nature and source of this resistance remains mysterious. Could they be the remnants of republican guards upset over being fired by Bremer? Administration officials have described the Baghdad bombers variously as "terrorists", "Saddam loyalists", or even Saddam himself. Rumsfeld himself called them "deadenders, foreign terrorists and criminal gangs". About Saddam himself, he was supposed to have said: "He's either dead, or he's incapacitated, or he's healthy and cowering in some tunnel someplace, trying to avoid being caught". Later, on October 26, Tom Friedman of the

New York Times would put it to Baghdad pro-consul Paul Bremer in CBS News' Face the Nation: "Who are these guys? Are they Syrians, Saudis, terrorists? Are they Iraqis, disgruntled soldiers, Ba'athists? Who are they"? To which Bremer replied: "All of the above, plus, of course, common criminals". "We've got three kinds of people that are a concern to us. First are the ex-Saddam killers, the killers of the Fedayeen Saddam and the intelligence agency. We've captured and killed quite a few of them. Secondly, we've got common criminals. As you know, Saddam let a lot of these guys go, and they're convicted murderers and rapists and torturers. And we've captured a number of them. And thirdly, we have terrorists, foreign terrorists." Yet, there remains a small chance that these people could be Iraqis fed up with the occupation. On October 27, Bush called the bombers "desperate ... killers ... [who] can't stand the thought of a free society." And after the late October carnage, defence department officials charged that Saddam may be "Saddam may be behind some of the attacks, or coordinating them or leading them", "somehow instigating or fomenting some of the resistance".

Occupation begets resistance, and resistance cripples reconstruction. Not ending wars swiftly can be very costly. The war in Iraq after Bush's tailhook landing was costing $1 billion per day. (Actually, it's $12,000 per second, $366,000,000 per 8-hours, or $1.1. billion per day, according to estimates computed by War Resisters League, using published federal budgetary data.) The US Congress is unwilling to finance the cost of maintaining the US occupation; why should anyone expect it to finance reconstruction? It was upset over the administrations request for nearly $87 billion (out of which $20.3 billion was for Iraq reconstruction) in September, but had to give in eventually: "It's like your building is half built, and the contractor comes in and says that to finish the building and put the roof on, it's going to cost a lot more", said Rep. Scott McInnis, R-Colo., a Bush ally. "What's your choice? You've got to put the roof on".

But the House exacted its revenge when it cut $1.7 billion of the $20.3 billion requested specifically for Iraqi reconstruction; the deleted items included a maternity hospital, two maximum-security prisons and 40 garbage trucks.

Administration officials earlier had asserted that Iraq's oil could largely finance its own reconstruction. But there was a catch. Thanks to sabotage, oil revenues are not pouring into the US authority in Iraq's coffers as fast as the Shiite militants pouring into the streets of Basra.

Oil production will be back to pre-war levels by May 2004. Not all things are bad. By November 2003, the Iraqi police force has swelled to 85,000 citizens, 85 per cent of Iraqi towns are under their own administration by municipal councils, electricity generation has risen by 25 per cent.

Alas, some things cannot be reconstructed and recovered. These real spoils of the war might have gone to mobs as well as organized gangs roaming the streets of Baghdad, amidst the chaos of the war as US troops were busily defending, among other things, the Iraqi oil ministry. For example, treasures were looted from the museums (at least one in ten of the objects in Iraq's national museum, if its director Dr Nawalaal Mutawalli is to be believed, totalling some 13,000 objects. Some have since been recovered, including 10 out of 42 pieces that were stolen from public galleries.).

Books in Iraq's libraries did better. According to an investigation by the British Library: The collections of the Library of the Iraqi Museum: one of the finest collections on history and archaeology of the Middle East were evacuated before the war started and protected, as were the Islamic Manuscripts Collection of the Iraqi Museum (about 4,000). The National Library of Iraq: about 500,000 printed books and serials, including 5,000 rare books, was all looted and burnt, as were the collections of the National Archives of Iraq containing documents from the Ottoman period onwards. The contents of the Saddam Manuscripts House, about 38,000 volumes, were evacuated before the war.

Perhaps the war will end one day, depending on how soon there emerge a truly indigenous government in Iraq, when Saddam (and hopefully Osama) has been captured, when oil starts flowing again in large quantities, and when the Baathists and republican guards have adapted to the new economy, if not as dashing new entrepreneurs or venture capitalists, then at least as tour guides and travel agents (provided anything is left for foreign tourists to see). The airport remains closed as of this writing, but the number of travel agencies in Baghdad has gone up. And, as an American friend of mine would add:

when there has been regime change in Washington. (In his view, this is a war caused by the Florida hanging chads, the US Supreme Court, and Al Gore's refusal to let Bill Clinton assume a higher profile role in the last presidential elections.)

Personally, however, I think the question of when the war will end is an emotional issue. Consider the finding of a recent survey conducted by the Pew Research Center based in Washington, DC:

> Despite an initial outpouring of public sympathy for America following the September 11, 2001 terrorist attacks, discontent with the United States has grown around the world over the past two years. Images of the US have been tarnished in all types of nations: among longtime NATO allies, in developing countries, in Eastern Europe and, most dramatically, in Muslim societies.

Using a US State Department poll from 2000 as a benchmark, the Pew survey involved more than 38,000 people in 44 nations. It reported that the favourable rating for America has dropped in 19 of the 27 nations surveyed by the State Department two years ago. While the US and its citizens continue to be rated positively by majorities in 35 of the 42 countries in which the question was asked, "True dislike, if not hatred, of America is concentrated in the Muslim nations of the Middle East and in Central Asia, today's areas of greatest conflict." According to Carroll Doherty, editor at the Pew Research Center, "In the Muslim world, it's pretty bleak ... [In] those nations with predominantly Muslim populations and countries that are key in the war on terrorism—Egypt, Pakistan, Turkey—the US image is pretty bad." Some figures are revealing: six per cent of Egyptians and 10 per cent of Pakistanis maintain a positive image of America. In five nations, Turkey, Jordan, Lebanon, Argentina and Bangladesh, a majority of people have an unfavourable opinion of the US. (We don't know about China, because survey workers were banned by the governments from asking questions about the US. In Saudi Arabia, Iraq, Iran and North Korea, researchers were denied permission to survey people.)

In Turkey, the number of people who had an unfavourable opinion of the United States rose to 83 per cent from 55 per cent a year ago, while in Indonesia, it is 83 per cent compared to 75 per cent in 2000.

In five Muslim countries—Indonesia, Jordan, Morocco, Pakistan and the Palestinian Authority—Osama bin Laden was chosen as one of the three political leaders they would most trust to "do the right thing" in world affairs. According to Andrew Kohut, director of the Pew Research Center, "Anti-Americanism has deepened, but it has also widened", he said. "You now find it in the far reaches of Africa—in Nigeria, among Muslims—and in Indonesia. People see America as a real threat. They think we're going to invade them".

If those trends are true, then the Iraq war, may never be over until America is loved again around the world. In the meantime, the killings continue on both sides. As Rumsfeld would say: "In a long hard war, we are going to have tragic days".

Sources

Straits Times, November 4, 2003.

https://listhost.uchicago.edu/pipermail/iraqcrisis/2003–May/000093.html; http://www.iht.com/articles/98398.html.

http://www.foxnews.com/story/0,2933,97527,00.html.

http://news.bbc.co.uk/2/hi/entertainment/3054974.stm.

http://edition.cnn.com/2003/WORLD/meast/07/03/iraq.museum/.

http://www.newsmax.com/archives/articles/2002/12/6/64838.shtml;.

Straits Times, November 3, 2003, p. 1.

The Economist, November 1, 2003, p. 45; www.commondreams.org.

http://www.spiked-online.com/Articles/00000006D9F9.htm>.

http://abcnews.go.com/sections/world/Primetime/iraq_main030409.html.

http://www.casperstartribune.net/articles/2003/04/27/news/casper/5e71ac71c5a3ea5263ee00209d7d4380.txt>.

http://www.cbsnews.com/stories/2003/10/27/ftn/main580231.shtml.

http://in.rediff.com/news/2003/oct/27iraq1.htm>.

http://www.nytimes.com/2003/10/31 politics31INTE.html?ex=1068569914&ei=1&en=cfa29c0c92bc8d8f>.

http://www.internationalism.org/inter/125_austerity.html.

http://www.twincities.com/mld/twincities/news/special_packages/iraq/6695132.htm.

http://www.washingtonpost.com/wp-dyn/articles/A43639-2003Oct17.html.

32

The Age of Fear: A Year After Iraq

"He was caught like a rat", gloated Major General Raymond Odierno, the commander of US the Army's 4th Infantry Division which helped capture the fallen Iraqi leader Saddam Hussein about nine miles from his hometown of Tikrit. That was on December 13, 2003. A day later, Defense Secretary Donald Rumsfeld joined in. In an interview with CBS News' 60 Minutes, he mused: "[H]ere was a man who was photographed hundreds of times shooting off rifles and showing how tough he was, and in fact, he wasn't very tough, he was cowering in a hole in the ground, and had a pistol and didn't use it and certainly did not put up any fight at all". On that occasion, Rumsfeld even allowed himself to be a little optimistic about the situation in Iraq. Since Saddam was "found with a sizable amount of money", this might mean the ability of "the Saddam Hussein family and his clique" in "providing money to people to go out and engage in acts against the coalition and the Iraqi people" had "ended".

Bush himself was more cautious. In his televised address to the nation on December 14, he reminded that Saddam's capture did not "mean the end of violence in Iraq. We still face terrorists who would rather go on killing the innocent than accept the rise of liberty in the heart of the Middle East".

While the realism was reassuring, it was also ironic. For if Saddam's capture did not end the terrorist carnage in Iraq, why was he being blamed for the anarchy that followed the conquest of Baghdad by American troops? In truth, the invasion of Iraq had opened up a brand new front in the war on terror. Dominique de Villepin, the French Foreign Minister, put it starkly: "Terrorism did not exist in Iraq before the war. Today, the country is one of the world's principal sources of world terrorism."

The bombings in Madrid in March 2004 were a powerful reminder that the downfall of Saddam has not dampened terrorism outside of Iraq either. Not surprisingly, a year after the invasion of Iraq, compelling doubts have emerged over Bush's handling of terrorism. Richard Clarke, once the top anti-terrorism adviser to Bush who was involved in all major meetings to plan America's response to the September 11 attacks, found it "outrageous" that Bush would be "running for re-election on the grounds that he's done such great things about terrorism." ("He ignored it. He ignored terrorism for months, when maybe we could have done something to stop 9/11. Maybe. We'll never know".)

Moreover, a year after Iraq, there has been little to show for measures to address the root causes of terror. Even such an ardent Iraq war apologist as *The Economist*, concedes that any political gains from the victory in Iraq, such as America' s changing relations with Iran, Libya and Syria, have been "overshadowed ... by the complete lack of progress in pacifying the region's most bitter conflict": that between the Palestinians and the Israelis.

Instead, the American response to terrorism continues to focus heavily on surveillance and securitization. And in that process, a year after Iraq, fear continues to trump freedom.

A good example of what's going on in the war on terror could be gleaned from page A4 of the *Boston Globe* of March 16, 2004. When I picked up a copy at the airport, three articles on that page caught my attention. The first one was a report on the Total Information Awareness programme, initiated by the Pentagon in response to the September 11 attacks. Part of this programme was an advanced data-mining programme developed by retired Admiral John Poindexter, a National Security Adviser to President Reagan who was fired over his unsavoury conduct in the Iran-Contra scandal. This software could scan government and commercial records for advance warning of terrorist attacks, warning signs which might include a sudden jump in school absenteeism or even the sale of orange juice in grocery stores. These, apparently, hold possible clues to an impending bio-terror attack. Faced with an outcry over its impact on privacy, Congress last year closed Poindexter's office in the Pentagon's Advanced Research and Development Activity outfit. But it allowed research into advanced data-mining by the US intelligence agencies, while cutting off funds for the development of privacy software that would hide the personal identities of people under surveillance like those involved in the orange juice transactions.

The second news item concerned the US Army Intelligence and Security Command seeking information on civilian participants in a

University of Texas conference on Islam ("Islam and the Law: The Question of Sexism"). The request was turned down. A third report was about the conviction of a professor named Sami Al-Arian in Florida. The professor had been accused of using a charity and an academic think-tank as a front to raise money for the Palestinian Islamic Jihad.

Whatever the merits of the professor's indictment, the first two reports are a scary reminder of the rise of the homeland security state in the Age of Fear. After Madrid, trains and railways stations are added to planes and airports, ships and seaports, as the kind of high value terrorist targets that need to be secured at all costs. But where will it end? There is little indication that security responses alone are killing off terrorism. As Richard Clarke put it, referring to an internal Pentagon memo by Rumsfeld which noted how extremist America haters are emerging faster than the US could capture or kill them, "[w]hatever we do to the original members of Al-Qaeda, a new generation of terrorists similar to them is growing. So, in addition to placing more cameras on our subway platforms, maybe we should be asking why the terrorists hate us. If we do not focus on the reasons for terrorism as well as the terrorists, the body searches we accept at airports may be only the beginning of life in the new fortress America".

In reality, the greatest threat to world peace in the 21st century comes not from terrorism, but the continued erosion, thanks to a narrowly focused and single minded war on terror that does little to address its fundamental causes, of America's legitimacy as a global leader. An America which cannot inspire the respect and willing cooperation of other nations, makes the world a much more dangerous place than it was before the war on terror was launched by the Bush administration.

Indications of the erosion of American legitimacy came in a Pew survey of America's image released on March 18, 2004 covering eight countries: France, Germany, Russia, Poland, Italy, Spain, Russia, and Britain. Apart from the first three, the rest are members of the coalition of the willing in Iraq. The survey found: "criticisms of U.S. foreign policy are almost universal. Overwhelming majorities disapprove of President Bush's foreign policy and the small boost he received in the wake of September 11 has disappeared." And what is even more significant is that the negative sentiments about Bush were despite the majority of those polled viewing the toppling of Saddam as something that will make the Iraqis better off and Middle East more stable.

One unfortunate by-product of the Iraq war is the damage to America's credibility in articulating its vulnerability to future threats posed by the proliferation of weapons of mass destruction. This was because the primary justification for the war has been completely shattered. To be sure, Bush has retreated (much earlier than Blair, who would not concede that the banned weapons might never be found until July 2004) somewhat from his persistent claim that Saddam's alleged possession of weapons of mass destruction was a genuine *causes belli*. He had little choice, especially after the final report by David Kay, the man in charge of surveying post-invasion Iraq for such weapons. Until then, Bush and Blair were insisting that Kay's Iraq Survey Group had unearthed some evidence of such weapons and more would be uncovered. Kay put paid to that line. He told a Senate hearing on January 28, 2004: "Let me begin by saying, we were almost all wrong, and I certainly include myself here". In an interview to the *Guardian*, Kay said: "I was convinced and still am convinced that there were no stockpiles of weapons of mass destruction at the time of the war". Any weapons the Iraqis might have possessed had probably been destroyed before 1998. "There were continuing clandestine activities but increasingly driven more by corruption than driven by purposeful directed weapons programmes". Bush quickly switched to Kay's formulation of "weapons of mass destruction-related programme activities", as opposed to "weapon stockpiles", to characterize what had been found in Iraq. This was in his 2004 state of the union speech in January. Yet Cheney and Rumsfeld continued to cast doubts over Kay's findings, paying scant regard to the Chief Weapons Inspector's final word of advice to the Bush administration that it should try to regain public trust by "confronting and coming clean with the American people, not just slipping a phrase into the state of the union speech".

It's a sad commentary on the world in which we live that the legitimacy of the first major war of the 21st century has come to rest on the difference between "weapons of mass destruction-related programme activities" and "weapon stockpiles." The WMD saga raises another important question: will people believe their governments the next time it seeks to justify a military mission as a counter-proliferation drive? A WMD attack by terrorists remains a real possibility, but this threat is not addressed by invading a country which had none of it (after the 1991 war and sanctions) and rewarding one (Pakistan) which not only had such weapons, but was spreading it around to anyone who could pay for it in the clandestine market. What credibility would a policy of fighting the WMD threat have when one country (a military dictatorship) is invaded for non-possession of WMDs, but another (also a military dictatorship), is rewarded with "major non-NATO ally status" for being a genuine proliferater?

Consistency and veracity in the war on terror are not the only casualties of the Iraq war. Another potential victim is democratic accountability. In an attack on his democratic rival in the 2004 presidential elections, Bush noted that while his critics "now agree that the world is better off with Saddam Hussein out of power; they just didn't support removing Saddam from power. May be they were hoping he'd lose the next Iraqi election." Smart joke, but a scary one too, because elections are no longer being seen as a legitimate means of political change, especially in the aftermath of the terrorist bombings in Madrid.

On March 11, 2004, terrorist attacks on three railway stations in Madrid led to the killing of more than 200 people and injury to over a thousand, Spain's worst carnage from a terrorist attack since the Spanish civil war which ended 65 years ago. Assessing the impact of these attacks on the general elections due to be held three days later, *The Economist* predicted that the ruling conservative party was "even more likely to win." But the Spanish electorate knew better and threw out the Aznar government, out of anger and resentment over its support for the war in Iraq and its deceptive handling of information about who actually had committed the bombings. This sparked outrage among the proponents of the war on terror. Edward Luttwak wrote of the "shameful downfall" of the Spanish people for having allowed a "small band of terrorists to dictate the outcome of their national elections". The Speaker of the US House of Representatives Dennis Hastert denounced the appeasement of terrorists.

While the Spanish electorate was being blamed by the intellectual elite for appeasing terrorists, ordinary mortals like Marlene Littwin, a retired social worker from New York City, finds another reason for the surge of terrorism around the globe. "Our government has been wrong on all of the important issues. Saddam had nothing to do with Osama bin Laden, there were no weapons of mass destruction, and we're inviting the same kind of terrorist acts that happened in Spain".

The outcome of the election in Spain does mean something important, and this has nothing to do with appeasement of the terrorist. It should be a lesson to governments if they indulge themselves in *illegal* wars against the wishes of their own people. This speaks well of the ability of democracies to exercise self-control on matters pertaining to use of force. Had the Aznar government done a better job of legitimizing the war, such as by seeking the UN mandate (as its successor now promises to do), by offering a credible rationale for the use of force, and by convincing its people that all other means to resolving the problem had been exhausted, then the Madrid attacks would have helped it to win re-election, as *The Economist*, had hoped for.

After Aznar, will it be Bush? Comparisons are already being made between George W. Bush and Sir Winston Churchill, who as Prime Minister of Britain won World War II, but lost the next general elections. But the comparison is misplaced. Churchill did not lead his country to war over a false pretext. Even if Bush and Blair did not deliberately manipulate intelligence about Iraq's WMD programme, they had a moral obligation to ensure that reports about the programme were verified as thoroughly as possible before it was used to justify a war. And Bush might still win the presidential election of 2004.

Fortunately, a year after Iraq, a real battle over the ideological soul of America has emerged. After scoring in Iraq, the neo-cons' star appears to have stopped rising. The neo-cons were angered by Bush's welcome for Chinese premier Wen Jiabao in the White House and his warning to Taiwan against declaring independence. This clearly goes against the neo-con plans for East Asia. Even more galling is the administration's welcoming of Libya into the community of "civilized" nations. To be sure, down as they may seem, the neo-cons are certainly not out. They continue to enjoy the support of the Christian conservatives and nationalists that form the Republican Party's popular base. But at least over Iraq, the neo-cons are put on the defensive. The Bush administration's decision to seek a UN Security Council resolution endorsing the occupation in the wake of the bombing of UN HQ in Iraq in August 2003 and the subsequent bombing in Najaf that killed the Ayatollah Baqir al-Hakim, undermined the neo-con goal of finish off the UN by ignoring it. The administration's request in September 2003 for $189 billion in military and reconstruction funding was an admission that there is no such thing as regime change on the cheap, as the neo-cons had made us believe. The decision to move towards a provisional government on an accelerated timetable, made by the administration in November 2003 when Paul Bremer's was suddenly recalled to Washington in November was another setback.

Meanwhile, a credible challenger has emerged in the US to the neo-con ideology. John Kerry's swift confirmation as the Democratic Presidential candidate has brought to the fore a real foe of the Bush imperium. "[h]ow is it possible to do what the Bush administration has done in Iraq: win a great military victory yet make America weaker", Kerry wonders. Kerry does not renounce the use of force. According to a *Time* magazine report, Kerry had apparently supported US military actions in Grenada, Panama, Kosovo and Afghanistan. Kerry might have gone to war against Saddam, but only because "we had exhausted the remedies of inspection." Kerry criticizes the Bush Doctrine, not the pre-emption aspect per se, which "we are always entitled to do ... under the charter of the U.N., which gives the right of self-defense of a nation". Rather he attacks "the extension of it by the Bush Administration to remove a person they don't like". Kerry asserts that Bush's "foreign policy of triumphalism fuels the fire of jihadists." The conduct of the Iraq war and the show of US might has "encouraged street level anger" in the Muslim World and might have "encouraged recruitment of terrorists". Kerry criticizes the Bush administration's disdain for the UN not because he is an idealist, but on practical grounds. "The legitimacy of the governing process that emerges from an essentially American process is always subject to greater questioning than one that is developed with broader, global consent". Involving the UN and NATO would ensure that the US would not have to shoulder the burden of Iraqi reconstruction alone.

A Kerry win may not immediately reverse the damage done by the policies of the Bush administration and the institutions. These will take time to unravel. In some cases, they might have already become permanent. But a return to multilateralism, a more sincere attempt to address the causes of terror, and a more principled use of force abroad and surveillance at home will help restore America's legitimacy as the pre-eminent world power. And that's really what the future of our world depends on.

Postscript: Ending the Age of Fear

After September 11, 2001, the world has been witnessing an American-led war on terror on two main fronts: a global struggle against the Al-Qaeda network; and a more specific campaign to destroy the Saddam Hussein regime in Iraq on the pretext of its alleged possession of weapons of mass destruction. The Bush administration claimed the two fronts to be one and the same. It failed to convince. In 2004, as the United States headed to its Presidential elections, the war on terror entered a critical turning point, with reasons for both despair and hope.

In April 2004, the US State Department, in its annual report on Patterns of Global Terrorism, claimed a sharp fall in the number of terrorist incidents. The Bush administration presented this as 'clear evidence' that the US was 'prevailing in the fight' against terrorism. But in June, the State Department admitted to a major error: what had really happened is that the incidence of terror had reached a 20-year high.[1] The war over Iraq had not only not dampened acts of terrorism, but might have aggravated it; as evidence suggests, the Madrid bombings were not carried out by Al-Qaeda but by a group of people angered by the attack on Iraq and the conduct of US policy against terrorism.

In May 2004, the world was shocked by the revelation of prisoner abuse at the Abu Ghraib jail. The picture showed a woman US officer dragging a prisoner on the neck on a leash, prisoners being intimidated by snarling dogs, a hooded Iraqi being threatened with electrocution. Rumsfeld resisted demands to resign to sooth Arab and international opinion. Bush administration officials let it be known that the President had taken Rumsfeld 'to the woodshed' over the tortures, but he also described him as a 'superb' Defense Secretary, while Vice President Dick Cheney described Rumsfeld as 'the best Secretary of Defense the United States has ever had.'[2]

Despite initial attempts by the Bush administration to dismiss these cases as the doings of a 'few rotten apples', a more deep-rooted basis for the tortures came to the light in June 2004, with the leaking of a legal opinion memo written by a US justice department official in

August 2002 which justified the use of torture, by narrowing the legal definition of torture that would exclude such acts as holding a person's head under water, by claiming that the president could not be constrained by the law against abuse in times of war, and that torturers, whose goal was to extract information (as opposed to simply intended to inflict pain) could claim immunity. The 'one lawyer' in the Justice Department's Office of the Legal Counsel who authored this opinion was appointed to a lifelong federal judgeship by the President.

The handover of sovereignty in Iraq on 28th June, brought forward two days for security reasons, was not the jubilant event with cheering crowds and stirring slogans that Bush's war cabinet would have dreamed of when the war was launched more than a year ago. The past century has seen many a legal, peaceful and orderly transfer of sovereignty from a colonial power to the government of a newly independent nation. This was an unlike any of them, what with the haste with which the American pro-consul, Paul Bremmer, fled Baghdad after a hasty handover ceremony in an undisclosed location.

In July 2004, the Select Committee on Intelligence of the United States Senate released a report on its investigation into prewar intelligence assessments on Iraq. The report concluded that the major key judgments in the Intelligence Community's October 2002 National Intelligence Estimate (NIE) 'either overstated, or were not supported by, the underlying intelligence reporting.'[3] These judgments included claims regarding Iraq 'reconstituting its nuclear program', being already in possession of 'chemical and biological weapons', developing unmanned aerial delivery systems for biological warfare agents, and actively continuing and advancing on its pre-1991 program of research, development, production and weaponization of an offensive biological weapons program. The committee did not find that the administration had knowingly misled the nation to war by cooking up and manipulating intelligence. But several people in the intelligence community reported that they had been put under pressure by tactics such as 'repetitive tasking' (asking the same questions again and again) aimed at eliciting the desired response.

A few days later, Britain's own investigation into prewar intelligence on Iraq carried out by Lord Butler found that intelligence was 'insufficiently robust', but absolved the Blair government of 'deliberate distortion' of intelligence and found that 'no single individual is to blame' for the intelligence failure. If this was an honest mistake, it implicated the Blair government of failing to do a thorough, honest and dispassionate evaluation of the intelligence and undermined the 'credibility' of the government. As the leader of the opposition in Britain, Michael Howard, pointed out, who would believe the government when it asks the nation to go to war in the future?

Not surprisingly, on July 5, 2004, the *International Herald Tribune* summed up international reactions to the war in Iraq and the revelations concerning Abu Ghraib with a headline 'U.S. moral ground takes a beating.' This echoed my 2002 opinion piece, 'One Result: The Decline of Liberal Democracy', which had argued that '[t]he US has lost its moral high ground in the global human rights debate.'

But amidst the darkening clouds of the Age of Fear, there have also been rays of hope.

As the fallout of the Abu Ghraib continued to reverbate around the world, the US Senate passed an amendment to the defence budget that would require the President to abide by the Geneva Conventions, account for all prisoners who have been denied POW status and 'expeditiously prosecute' cases of terrorism to avoid the 'indefinite detention of prisoners'.

On June 28 2004, the US Supreme Court backed the Bush administration's right to hold prisoners (both American and foreigners) without trial in Guantanamo Bay, but ruled against the Bush administration's decision to deny them recourse to US courts (on the pretext that they were being held outside the territory of the US). It affirmed such prisoners' right to due process of law and to speedy and public trial.

The Bush administration seems to have begun an effort to repair relations with the UN and the Old Europe. The UN was involved in the effort to create the Iraqi leadership to receive formal handover of sovereignty. The US President visited Europe to celebrate Europe's liberation from Nazi rule and attended a NATO summit where the decision was taken to get the alliance involved in training Iraqi security forces.

James Mann, author of *The Rise of the Vulcans: The History of Bush's War Cabinet* proclaimed the neo-cons to be a 'spent force', with their core ideas such as preemption and axis of evil formulation losing shine over continuing post-invasion Iraqi instability, the continuing impasse in the Middle East peace process, the revelations of torture.[4]

In July, the government of the Philippines pulled out its troops from Iraq to comply with the demands of the kidnappers of a Filipino truck driver. It acted to avoid widespread popular anger which would have confronted the government had the worker been beheaded, as his captors had threatened. It also showed a certain disjunction between the Manila government's definition of its 'national interest', the basis of its decision in joining the coalition of the willing, and the interests of the people. From Madrid to Manila, governments are waking up to their domestic opinion in the war on terror. As I had noted in 'Terrorism and Democracy', this may be the most important factor shaping how the international community responds to the September 11 attacks.

The change in the government in India showed that joining the stronger side in the war on terror does not win votes if the ordinary people remain in economic misery. Possible changes in government in Australia and Britain, not to mention the United States, induced by popular disillusionment with the way these governments have conducted the war on terror, could reshape how the world fights terror, and at what cost.

Ending the Age of Fear depends very much on how far these developments go in reining in America's neo-imperial instincts. It requires a future American administration (whether headed by George W. Bush or John F. Kerry)—before it commits its forces to a foreign war—to be truthful to its own people and the international community about the real justification for the war, and taking firm measures to prevent its military forces from committing further acts of torture. It depends on the governments of the world striking a balance between fear and freedom, between counter-terrorism measures and civil liberties. It also requires eschewing unilateral measures to combat terrorism, and making sincere efforts at multilateral cooperation, rather than succumbing to the self-serving convenience of the coalition of the willing.

Endnotes

1 Paul Krugman, 'White House Claims on Terrorism Don't Add Up', International Herald Tribune, June 26–27, 2004, p. 5.

2 'A Ghastly Week', The Economist, July 15, 2006, pp. 29–31.

3 Report on The U.S. Intelligence Community's Prewar Intelligence Assessments on Iraq, Select Committee on Intelligence, United States Senate, available at http://intelligence.senate.gov.

4 James Mann, Bush's Team Has Only a Spent Vision', Financial Times July 8, 2004, p. 13.

Sources

"America's Image Further Erodes, Europeans Want Weaker Ties", March 18, 2003, http://people-press.org/reports/display.php3?ReportID=175.

CBS News, 60 Minutes, March 24, 2004, http://www.cbsnews.com/stories/2004/03/19/60minutes/main607356.shtml.

Edward Luttwak, "Shame on Spain", March 16, 2004, http://www.globeandmail.com/servlet/ArticleNews/TPPrint/LAC/20040316/COLUTT16/TPComment/

Guardian http://www.guardian.co.uk, March 3, 2004.

Los Angeles Times, March 21, 2004, A11.

http://www.cnn.com/2003/WORLD/meast/12/14/sprj.irq.main/.

Paul Krugman, 'White House Claims on Terrorism Don't Add Up', *International Herald Tribune*, June 26–27, 2004, p. 5.

'A Ghastly Week', *The Economist*, July 15, 2006, pp. 29–31.

Report on The U.S. Intelligence Community's Prewar Intelligence Assessments on Iraq, Select Committee on Intelligence, United States Senate, available at http://intelligence.senate.gov.

James Mann, Bush's Team has Only a Spent Vision', *Financial Times* July 8, 2004, p. 13.

The 9/11 Commission Report, http://a257.g.akamaitech.net/7/257/2422/05aug20041050/www.gpoaccess.gov/911/pdf/fullreport.pdg

"9/11 Panel Report: 'We Must Act'", July 23, 2004, http://www.cnn.com/

ACLU Press Release, July 22, 2004, http://www.aclu.org/

Richard Clarke, "The New Terrorist Threat", *Time*, March 22, 2004.

"Twilight of the Neocons?" December 23, 2003, http://billmon.org/archives/000924.html; *Boston Globe*, March 16, 2004.

Time, March 15, 2004.

"U.S. Appeasement Warning to Spain", *Yahoo News*, March 18, 2004, http://uk.news.yahoo.com/040318/325/eouqr.html.

Further Reading

Acharya, Amitav. 1997. "Beyond Anarchy: Third World Instability and International Order after the Cold War". In Stephanie Neumann, ed. *International Relations Theory and the Third World.* New York: St Martin's Press.

Alexander, Yonah (ed.). 2003. *Combating Terrorism: Strategies of Ten Countries.* Ann Arbor, MI: University of Michigan Press.

Anwar Ibrahim. "Growth of Democracy is the Answer to Terrorism." *International Herald Tribune.* October 11, 2001.

Bajpai, Kanti. 2002. *The Roots of Terror.* New Delhi: Penguin Books.

Berman, Paul. 2003. *Terror and Liberalism.* W.W. Norton & Company.

Booth, Ken and Tim Dunne. 2002. *Worlds in Collision: Terror and the Future of Global Order.* Palgrave Macmillan.

Carr, Caleb. 2002. *The Lessons of Terror.* New York: Random House.

Carter, Ashton B., John Deutsch, and Philip Zelikow. 1998. "Catastrophic Terrorism: Tackling the New Danger." *Foreign Affairs* (November/December 1998).

Chalk, Peter. 1998. "The Response to Terrorism as a Threat to Liberal Democracy". *American Journal of Politics and History* 44: 3 (1998).

Chomsky, Noam. 1991. "International Terrorism: Image and Reality". In Alexander George, ed. *Western State Terrorism.* New York: Routledge.

Cole, David et al. 2002. *Terrorism and the Constitution: Sacrificing Civil Liberties in the Name of National Security.* New Press.

Crenshaw, Martha, ed. 1983. *Terrorism, Legitimacy and Power.* Middletown Conn.: Wesleyan University Press.

Desker, Barry and Kumar Ramakrishna. 2002. "Forging an Indirect Strategy in Southeast Asia", *The Washington Quarterly* 25:2 (Spring 2002).

Farish Noor. 2001. "Who Elected You, Mr Osama?" *Malaysiakini.com* 10 October 2001. Available at http://www.worldpress.org/asia/1201malaysiakini.com.

Friedman, Thomas L. 2003. *Longitudes and Attitudes: The World in the Age of Terrorism.* Anchor.

Fukuyama, Francis. 1992. *The End of History and the Last Man.* London: Penguin Books.

Grundy, Kenneth, and Michael Weinstein. 1974. *Ideologies of Violence.* Columbus, Ohio: Merrill.

Gunaratna, Rohan. 2003. *Terrorism in the Asia-Pacific: Threat and Response.* Singapore: Eastern University Press.

_______. 2002. *Inside Al Qaeda: Global Network of Terror.* New York: Columbia University Press.

Halliday, Fred. 2002. *Two Hours That Shook the World: September 11, 2001: Causes and Consequences.* London: Saqi Books.

Heymann, Philip B. 1998. *Terrorism and America: A Commonsense Strategy for a Democratic Society.* Cambridge, Massachusetts: MIT Press.

Hoffman, Bruce. 1999. *Inside Terrorism.* New York: Columbia University Press.

Hoffmann, Stanley. 2003. "America Goes Backwards". *New York Review of Books* 50:20 (June 12, 2003).

Hoge, James F., Jr. and Gideon Rose (eds.) 2001. *How Did This Happen? Terrorism and the New War.* New York: Public Affairs.

Homer-Dixon, Thomas. 2002. "The Rise of Complex Terrorism". *Foreign Policy.* January 2002.

Howard, Russell D. and Reid L. Sawyer. 2003. *Terrorism and Counter Terrorism: Understanding the New Security Environment.* Connecticut: McGraw-Hill.

Hudson, Rex et al. 1999. *Who Becomes a Terrorist and Why: The 1999 Government Report on Profiling Terrorists.* Guilford, Conn.: Lyons Press.

Huntington, Samuel P. 2001 "The Age of Muslim Wars", *Newsweek* (Special Edition December 2001).

Huntington, Samuel P. 1997. *The Clash of Civilizations and the Remaking of World Order.* New York: Touchstone Books.

International Crisis Group, 2002., *Indonesia Backgrounder: How the Jemaah Islamiyah Terrorist Group Operates*, Asia Report No. 43. Jakarta: December 11, 2002.

Kagan, Robert. 2002. "Power and Weakness". *Policy Review*, No. 113 (June and July).

_______ 2003. *Of Paradise and Power: America and Europe in the New World Order.* New York: Knopf

Kahler, Miles. 2002. "Networks and Failed States: September 11 and the Long Twentieth Century." Paper presented for the Annual Meeting of the American Political Science Association, Boston, MA.

Kapstein, Ethan B. and Michael Mastanduno, eds. 1999. *Unipolar Politics: Realism and State Strategies after the Cold War.* New York: Columbia University Press.

Kegley, Charles W. Jr., ed. 2003. *The New Global Terrorism: Characteristics, Causes, Controls*. Upper Saddle River, NJ: PrenticeHall.

Kepel, Gilles. 2002. *Jihad: The Trial of Political Islam*. Massachusetts: Harvard University Press.

Dennis Kux, *The United States and Pakistan 1947–2000: Disenchanted Allies.* Washington: Woodrow Wilson Center Press, 2001.

Laqueur, Walter. 1999. *The New Terrorism: Fanaticism and the Arms of Mass Destruction.* Oxford: Oxford University Press.

_______. 1987. *The Age of Terrorism.* Boston: Little Brown.

Larkin, Bruce. 2001. "Why This is Not a War, And Why It Is Important to Understand that This is Not a War." October 24, 2001. Unpublished commentary. http://www.learnworld.com/DRAFTS/DRAFT.2001.10.17.NotAWar.pdf.

Layne, Christopher. 1993. "The Unipolar Illusion: Why New Great Powers Will Rise". *International Security*. 17: 4 (Spring 1993).

Livingstone, Neil C. 1984. *The War against Terror.* London: Lexington Books.

Maerli, Morten Bremer. 2001. "The Threat of Nuclear Terrorism: Nuclear Weapons or Other Nuclear Explosive Devices." Presented at the IAEA Symposium on International Safeguards: Verification and Nuclear Material Security. Vienna, Austria. October 29– November 2, 2001.

William Maley., Ed. "Fundamentalism- Reborn? Afghanistan and the Taliban", London, Hurst and Company, Second Impression, 1999.

Nye, Joseph S. 2002. *The Paradox of American Power: Why the World's Only Superpower Can't Go it Alone.* Oxford: Oxford University Press.

Pape, Robert A. 2003. "The Strategic Logic of Suicide Terrorism". *American Political Science Review* 97:3 (August 2003).

Pillar, Paul. 2001. *Terrorism and U.S. Foreign Policy.* Washington, D.C.: Brookings.

Pitsuwan, Surin. 2001. "Islam in Southeast Asia: A Personal Viewpoint." *The Nation* September 22, 2001.

Raja Mohan. C. 2003. *Crossing the Rubicon: The Shaping of India's New Foreign Policy* (New Delhi: Viking)

Rapoport, David C. 1984. "Fear and Trembling: Terrorism in Three Religious Traditions." *American Political Science Review* 78:3 (September 1984).

Rashid, Ahmed. 2002. *Jihad: The Rise of Militant Islam in Central Asia.* New Haven: Yale University Press.

Ruggie, John Gerard. 1993. *Multilateralism Matters: The Theory and Practice of an Institutional Form.* New York: Columbia University Press.

Singapore, Ministry of Home Affairs. 2003. *The Jemmah Islamiyah Arrests and the Threat of Terrorism*, White Paper.

Sohl, Michael, and George Lopez, eds. 1986. *State Terrorism: An Agenda for Research*. Wesport, Conn. Greenwood Press.

Sopiee, Noordin, "What Is Terrorism? Who is a Terrorist? Why Terrorism?", Paper Presented at the 16th Asia Pacific Roundtable, Kuala Lumpur, June 2–5, 2002.

Tan, Andrew and Kumar Ramakrishna (eds.). 2002. *The New Terrorism: Anatomy, Trends and Counter-Strategies*. Singapore: Eastern Universities Press.

Thayer, Carlyle A. 2003. "The Bush-Howard Doctrines: Pulling Down the International System?" In *What's Next? (Future Directions International)* (September 2003).

The Library of Congress, Congressional Research Service. 2003. *International Terrorism in South Asia*, CRS Report for Congress, November 3.

Waltz, Kenneth. 1979. *Theory of International Politics*. Reading, MA: Addision-Wesley.

Weinberg, Leonard, and Paul Davis. 1989. *Introduction to Political Terrorism.* New York: McGraw-Hill.

Whittaker, David, ed. 2001. *The Terrorism Reader.* London: Routledge.

Wilkinson, Paul 2001. *Terrorism versus Democracy: the Liberal State Response.* London: Frank Cass.

Zakaria, Fareed. 2003. *The Future of Freedom: Illiberal Democracy at Home and Abroad.* W.W. Norton & Company.

How This Book Evolved

This book is written around a series of lectures and opinion pieces which I delivered and wrote in the aftermath of September 11, 2001, but especially in the months surrounding the war in Iraq. Several of these pieces have been previously published, in some abridged or expanded form. The remainder are based either on notes prepared for lectures in Singapore or America, reflections written in moments of anguish and reflection over the war. Most of these were never submitted for publication, but a few, such as they were duly turned down because they were "outdated" or otherwise unsuitable for the particular column they were intended. Of the published ones, I have tried to include original and uncut versions (keeping in mind most newspapers are loath to publish anything over 1000 words from an undistinguished writer). Of the unpublished entrees, I have made some modifications from the original lecture notes, mostly updating them.

"The Age of Fear" grew out of notes for an invited lecture at the Law Department of the National University of Singapore on February 5, 2003. It has been rewritten periodically since. **"Who is a Terrorist?"** was written soon after the publication of my article "One Lesson: The Retreat of Liberal Democracy" in the *International Herald Tribune* on September 17, 2002, followed by a BBC World Service interview where Owen Bennett-Jones grilled me on precisely the same question. I sent him the piece soon after the interview. **"Why this Was Not a Clash of Civilizations?"** was published by the *International Herald Tribune* on January 10, 2002 under the title "Clash of Civilizations? No, of Interests and Principles". **"Hatred, Harmony and the Causes of Terror"** was based on my summary notes of a session of Harvard University Asia Center's annual Asian Vision 21 Group meeting in Bangkok during May 9–11, 2002. **"The Fear of Islam"** is inspired by a dialogue on Islam between Singaporean and French (Centre Asie of IFRI, the French Institute of International Relations) scholars held in Singapore during November 10–11, 2003. **"Terror in Southeast Asia: Global or Local?"** draws from a lecture I gave to the University Seminar on Southeast Asia at Columbia University in New York on 6 March 2003. The two essays on South

Asia **"Pakistan: Riding the Terrorist Tiger"**, and **"The Many Faces of Terror in South Asia"** were written in December 2003 with a view to examine how the terrorism discourse in South Asia compares with that in Southeast Asia, and as a test of Huntington's overarching "clash of civilizations" framework. **"Palestinians as Terrorists"** grew out of an internal debate with colleagues in Singapore in the immediate aftermath of the attacks on the World Trade Center and the Pentagon over the question whether the Palestinian struggle justifies the World Trade Center attacks (it does not, in my view). It was updated in the wake of the collapse of the Bush "road map".

"Unipolar World,Unilateral Hegemon" was first written as a paper for the Southeast Asian Conflict Network meeting held in Penang on July 15–17, 2003; it also incorporates a lecture I gave to the Senior Commanders Course in Singapore. "1991 and 2001" was written just before the US forces attacked the Taliban. **"Dubya's Dangerous, Divisive Doctrine"** appeared in the *Straits Times* on October 16, 2002. The same paper on January 16, 2003 published **"Why A Second Gulf War is Not in Asia's Interest?"** under the title "The Second Gulf War: Why the US and Asia are a Gulf Apart". **"The War in Iraq: Morality or the National Interest?"**, appeared first in the *Commentary* series of the Institute of Defence and Strategic Studies, and was later published by the *Straits Times* on April 2, 2003. **"Fear, Power and Empire"** was delivered at a symposium on "Legal, Military and Moral Aspects of the War on Iraq," organized by the Institute of Southeast Asian Studies on April 9, 2003, at the thick of the war over Iraq. **"Coalition of the Willing or Coalition of the Coerced?"** was written in response to a request by the features editor of the *Straits Times* and appeared in the paper under the rather strange title "Will the US Let Others Form a Coalition of the Willing?" **"Debating the Gulf War"** was written as a contribution to the special website set up by the brave Melissa Kwee of The Education for Understanding Initiative, which invited me to speak at an inspired youth forum on "Perspectives on the War on Iraq" held on May 22, 2003. It was subsequently turned down by a Singapore newspaper for being outdated. **"How Will Mr Bush Run the World?"** appeared in the *Business Times* of Singapore on May 13, 2003 under the same title. **"Coping with American Power"** appeared in the *Japan Times*,

May 3, 2003, although a brutally edited shorter version had appeared in IHT as "Ripples of Iraq will Rock Asia".

"Terrorism and Democracy" is extracted from a longer essay titled: "State-Society Relations: Asia and the World after September 11", which I contributed to a volume *World's In Collision: Terror and the Future of Global Order* (London: Palgrave, 2002) edited by Ken Booth and Tim Dunne. The **"The Retreat of History?"** appeared as "One Result: The Retreat of Liberal Democracy" in IHT on September 17, 2002. **"From Fear to Freedom in the Arab World"** was written in two stages, the first after the US "victory" in Iraq and later after the Bush speech at the National Endowment for Democracy. It has never been submitted for publication. **"Fighting Terror in Southeast Asia"** is based on my lecture to the staff of the United Nations Department of Political Affairs in New York on March 4, 2003. **"Asia Between America and Europe"** was written as an assignment for my students at the University of Malaysia's Asia Europe Institute in January 2002 when I was a Visiting Professor there. The course was about Asian regional integration and I gave it to my students along with Kagan's original article in *Policy Review*. It was subsequently published by the *International Herald Tribune* on January 23, 2003, severely truncated and with a truly atrocious title: "Asians Wary of Pushy Outsiders". I was so embarrassed by the title that to this date, I only hand out the original version. **"Asia and the Bush Doctrine"** evolved from notes for a lecture at the Institute of Defence and Strategic Studies on "US Grand Strategy & A New International Order", delivered on May 23, 03. A longer version of this paper appeared in a special issue (vol. 27, no. 4, December 2003) of the journal *Asian Perspective*. "American Grand Strategy After the Gulf War", and. **"Terror and the Asian Balance of Power"** was written as a contribution to the Asian Innovation Forum in Bali on the theme of "Renewal, Renovation and Reconstruction in Asia", during March 15–18, 2003, where every participant was asked to write a short essay on a topic of their choice. **"India From Nehru to Curzon"** is an original essay for this volume, written around November 2003; the idea came from reading C. Raja Mohan's perceptive and detailed account of Indian foreign policy under the BJP regime. **"Howard's Corollary"** was a reaction to Australian Prime Minister John Howard's threat of using pre-emption to fight terrorism against Australia. It appeared in *Today* on December 20, 2002 under the title of "Friends and Neighbours". **"After Victory: An Opportunity for Global Order Reform"** soon after the fall of Saddam. **"When the War was (Not) Over"** was written in December 2003, as a commentary on the non-discovery of the weapons of mass destruction in Iraq and Bush-Blair's failure to follow up regime change with nation-building. **"The Age of Terror: A Year After Iraq"** was written in Singapore in March 2003 to reflect on the first anniversary of the launching of the US attack on Iraq. **"Waging the 'War on Terror'. Singapore's Responses and Dilemmas"** appears as a chapter in Arun Mahizhnan, ed. Singapore Perspectives 2004 (Singapore: Marshall Cavendish Academic, 2004).

www.ingramcontent.com/pod-product-compliance
Lightning Source LLC
LaVergne TN
LVHW050625100826
845148LV00011B/1734

* 9 7 8 0 4 1 5 7 3 2 9 1 8 *